Henry Cecil was the pseudoi
Leon. He was born in Norwood Green Rectory, near London, England in 1902. He studied at Cambridge where he edited an undergraduate magazine and wrote a Footlights May Week production. Called to the bar in 1923, he served with the British Army during the Second World War. While in the Middle East with his battalion he used to entertain the troops with a serial story each evening. This formed the basis of his first book, *Full Circle*. He was appointed a County Court Judge in 1949 and held that position until 1967. The law and the circumstances which surround it were the source of his many novels, plays, and short stories. His books are works of great comic genius with unpredictable twists of plot which highlight the often absurd workings of the English legal system. He died in 1976.

BY THE SAME AUTHOR
ALL PUBLISHED BY HOUSE OF STRATUS

NATURAL CAUSES

by

Henry Cecil

**HOUSE OF
STRATUS**

This edition published in 2000 by House of Stratus, an imprint of Stratus Holdings plc, 24c Old Burlington Street, London, W1X 1RL, UK.

www.houseofstratus.com

Typeset, printed and bound by House of Stratus.

A catalogue record for this book is available from the British Library.

ISBN 1-84232-058-0

Contents

CHAPTER ONE

Tame Solicitor

Some three years before the attempt was made to blackmail a High Court judge a young solicitor, Gilbert Swanley, walked into the offices of the London Clarion. Had he not done so the attempt would never have been made. Indeed, it would not have occurred to the blackmailer to make it. Yet Gilbert never met the judge and had not the remotest connection with him. It was simply that his was the earliest act to which the crime can be traced. In the same way you may owe your existence to some trifling events, such as the dropping of a stitch and consequent missing of a train; had they not occurred your father would never have met your mother. It was to that extent, and to that extent only, that Gilbert Swanley was responsible for the terrible dilemma which eventually faced a High Court judge, a judge of the highest reputation, publicly and privately, whose integrity was rightly unquestioned.

Gilbert Swanley had applied for the post of private solicitor to the Chairman and Managing Director of a company which owned a number of important newspapers, of which the *London Clarion* was the largest. In fact he had nearly withdrawn his application in view of quite an attractive proposal which was made to him by a firm of London solicitors. But the interview was offered while he was considering the solicitors' proposal and he decided to attend it before making up his mind. He walked into the offices of the *London Clarion*, said who he was, and was told to wait. To his surprise he had only been waiting a few minutes when he was shown into the office of the great man himself. Alexander Bean was a remarkable man. Starting as a newsboy he had eventually become the controller of some of the most influential newspapers in England. He was entirely self-educated, but, as part of his education, he had taken the trouble to acquire quite a cultivated voice. He was neither proud nor ashamed of starting as a newsboy. It was irrelevant. He was not one of those who think that the possession of a strong Cockney accent is an asset to a man in an important position. He was not in the least a snob. He simply had the fixed intention of succeeding at anything to which he put his hand. All opposition must be and would be overcome. He had great business acumen, he was not a gambler but would take extreme risks if the occasion appeared to justify his taking them and, in vital matters, he had never been proved wrong yet. In matters which he did not consider vital he would sometimes make mistakes, almost deliberately; the reason was simple; on such occasions he did not consider the pros and cons of the affair itself but only his own self-importance. He would, for example, consider it a vital matter that he should not be executed or go to prison, but, subject to that and any similar qualification, he would disregard the law entirely if he thought fit. Laws were made for smaller people, not for Alexander Bean. The exception was, of course, any law he made himself, and this could easily be changed without the necessity of lengthy proceedings in Parliament or the Law Courts. He was ruthless, generous, eccentric, and capable of immense hard work. He was inordinately vain; he firmly believed that there was no task too difficult for him to carry out successfully and he desired other people to think this too. He was quick to reward good service and quick to take offence. No one could be quite sure what he would do next. He knew that he had the reputation for giving sudden and wholly unexpected orders to his staff. He enjoyed this reputation. He was, in short, a true megalomaniac.

When Gilbert Swanley was shown into the great man's room Alexander Bean simply looked at him. The door was closed and the two of them were left alone, the Chairman sitting in his chair, Gilbert standing and wondering how the interview would begin. He was an able young man and, having regard to Mr Bean's reputation, was quite prepared for the conversation to proceed on unorthodox lines, but he proposed to take his cue from Mr Bean. So, while Mr Bean sat and looked at him standing, he stood and looked at Mr Bean sitting. If it's a game of who can keep up staring longest, he said to himself, I can play at that. He was, in fact, an expert and had been since childhood when he and his twin sister had practised it for what seemed in those days like hours. Eventually Mr Bean had to make the first move.

'Well?' he said.

'This is an interview for the purpose of your choosing a tame solicitor, sir. I am one of the applicants.'

'I see,' said Mr Bean, and relapsed into silence. Gilbert stood his ground and waited for the next cue. It came after three-quarters of a minute, actually timed by Mr Bean from his watch.

'Are you a solicitor?'

'Yes, sir.'

'Tame?'

'Within the meaning of the advertisement, yes. Otherwise, I should say no, sir.'

There was silence again. This had continued for an exact minute and a half when Mr Bean opened his mouth as though to speak and then closed it again without saying anything. Another minute went by. It was half past three. At this rate, thought Gilbert, I shall be late for the theatre; it starts at half past seven. Bearing in mind that he was taking Alice to the theatre and that she objected to his being late, Gilbert decided to make a move.

'Anything else you'd like to know about me, sir, or was my letter detailed enough?'

'Who asked you to speak?' said Mr Bean.

'No one, sir, but I got tired of doing nothing.'

'You like work then?'

'If it leads anywhere.'

'Are you aware that the *London Clarion* is read in one out of every four houses in England?'

'So it says, sir.'

'And that includes prefabricated houses.'

'I didn't know that, sir.'

'Well, you've learned something by coming here then.'

'Thank you very much, sir.'

'What for?'

'For telling me about the prefabricated houses.'

'That information did not interest you in the least.'

'No, sir.'

'Then why thank me?'

'I was at Winchester, sir.'

'Manners makyth Man, eh?'

'Were you there too, sir?'

'You know perfectly well I was not. I left school when I was fourteen. And let me tell you that manners do not make reporters, editors or newspaper proprietors.'

'I follow that, sir, but they're quite useful to tame solicitors.'

'Yes, you may have a point there. D'you know any law?'

'About as much as the average solicitor.'

'Well – you won't get the job on that.'

'Very well, sir. Thank you for seeing me.'

'I didn't say you wouldn't get the job. I said you wouldn't get it on the strength of your law. As a matter of fact, no one would. Damned few lawyers – barristers or solicitors – know any law, and the few that do wouldn't apply for this job. Let's see if you know anything. What's the difference between civil and criminal libel?'

'Broadly speaking, libel to be criminal must be calculated to lead to a breach of the peace.'

'Humph. Suppose I had an editor and wanted to fire him – what notice should I give him?'

'None.'

'You'll start tomorrow. £2,500 a year to begin with. Your office is upstairs. Use your initiative. Don't worry me with trifles. Don't do anything important without my approval. If you don't know the difference between what's a trifle and what's important, you'll be no use to me. Good afternoon.'

That evening Gilbert, in telling Alice that he had got the job, said that he thought he could hold it for six months if he lasted a week and for three years if he lasted six months. His prophecy turned out to be almost exactly correct. He lasted three years, although he had some difficulty in lasting the first week. He had only been there a few hours when the telephone rang.

'Legal Department?'

'Speaking.'

'This is Rounce and Ponsonby. Brown and Clarion Newspapers will be on tomorrow. Is Mr Bean going to give evidence?'

'I'm afraid I've only just taken over. I don't know the case. I'll turn it up and ring you back.'

Gilbert sent for the file containing the papers relating to the action of *Brown v Clarion Newspapers Ltd*. The file started with a somewhat one-sided correspondence. The first letter was from Mr Brown to Mr Bean.

'Dear Mr Bean,

I was most surprised when your secretary telephoned me that my services would no longer be required and that I was not to attend at the office any more. Might I have an explanation, please? Am I supposed to be dismissed? If so, why? In any event, I am entitled to notice and shall hold myself at your disposal pending hearing from you.

Yours sincerely,

ANDREW BROWN.'

The next letter was dated seven days later.

'Dear Mr Bean,

I have had no answer to my letter of the 2nd inst and must ask you to be good enough to let me have a reply. In particular, I must know whether you wish to make use of my services during the appropriate period of notice. Please let me have a definite answer by return.'

There was a reply to that letter. It was as follows:

'Dear Mr Brown,

Here is your definite answer. No.

Yours sincerely,

ALEXANDER BEAN.'

A few days later Mr Brown returned to the assault.

'Dear Mr Bean,

In view of your letter I am treating myself as wrongfully dismissed by your Company and I shall be glad to know what compensation you propose to offer me. I shall, of course, now seek other suitable employment, but, as you were well aware when you first employed me, mine is a rather specialised job and it is not easy to find vacancies.'

Fourteen days went by. Then:

'Dear Mr Bean,

'I really must ask you to answer my letter of the 15th inst. I am still without employment.

Yours faithfully,

ANDREW BROWN.'

There was a reply to that letter.

'Dear Mr Brown,

I am not surprised.

Yours sincerely,

ALEXANDER BEAN.'

Then came another from Mr Brown.

'Dear Mr Bean,

In view of your last offensive letter I am placing the whole matter in the hands of my solicitors.

Yours faithfully,

ANDREW BROWN.'

The next letter was from Mr Brown's solicitors.

'Dear Sir,

We have been consulted by our client Mr Andrew Brown in regard to his employment by your Company. Mr Brown was employed under an oral contract at a salary of £950 per annum. In view of the nature of his employment, we have advised him that he was entitled at the least to six months' notice of termination, but on the 31st March you caused him to be wrongfully dismissed without any notice at all. We have accordingly advised our client that he is entitled to claim as damages from you £475 less any sum he may be able to earn during the remainder of the six months. So far he has been unable to obtain any other employment. Please let us know that the claim is admitted and will be met. Otherwise we have advised our client that there is no alternative to issuing a writ against you.

Yours faithfully,
GROANER AND GROANER.'

There was no reply, and the next letter was again from Messrs Groaner and Groaner.

'Dear Sir,

Unless we receive a reply to our letter of the 18th inst within seven days, our instructions are to issue a writ and we shall be glad to have the name of solicitors who will accept service on your behalf.'

On the sixth day Messrs Groaner and Groaner received a reply.

'Dear Sirs,

Messrs Rounce and Ponsonby will.

Yours faithfully,
ALEXANDER BEAN.'

A writ had then been issued and, in due course, Messrs Rounce and Ponsonby had asked Mr Bean for a statement about the case. Mr Rounce himself called to see Mr Bean.

'I haven't much time,' said Mr Bean. 'What d'you want to know?'

'Have you any defence to the action?'

'Of course I have. The man was hopeless. Business efficiency expert, my foot. The office would have had to close down if we'd had him much longer.'

'Inefficiency is a very difficult ground on which to justify dismissal without notice.'

'It's no ground at all. I know all about the law of wrongful dismissal.' This was not strictly true, though in view of the large number of employees whom he had dismissed without reason or notice, Mr Bean had considerable experience of the situation.

'Then what is your defence?'

'Perfectly simple. Termination by mutual consent. All done by word of mouth. In this office. Day before he left. No one present except him and me.'

'He agreed to leave without notice?'

'Certainly.'

'Well – that is rather different.'

'Of course it is. I can't lose, can I?'

'Well, if the judge accepts your word – '

'*If* the judge accepts my word – really, Mr Rounce, that's a strange thing to say to me.'

'Well, of course, I accept it,' said Mr Rounce, not very happily, 'but I can't answer for every judge on the Bench.'

'I'm not asking you to do so. It's for the plaintiff to prove his case, isn't it? Well, if I say that we agreed to cancel his contract, that's an end of the matter, isn't it?'

'It's for you to prove that, as a matter of fact.'

'Rubbish. The plaintiff has to prove his case. I know a good bit more about the law than you chaps think.'

If Mr Bean had not been such an important client, Mr Rounce would probably have refused to act for him any longer, but his work was worth a very large annual sum to Messrs Rounce and Ponsonby, and so Mr Rounce had to make the best of it.

'It's a pity,' he went on, 'that you didn't mention this termination by mutual consent in any of your letters.'

'D'you think I've time to write long letters to every Tom, Dick and Harry who writes to me? Where d'you think the newspapers would be if I wasted time like that? Anyway, he never asked me if we'd agreed on termination by mutual consent. Why should I tell him?'

'Well, Mr Bean,' said Mr Rounce, untruthfully, 'I quite understand what you say, but,' he added, more truthfully, 'I'm afraid you're likely to be cross-examined a good bit by the plaintiff's counsel about those letters.'

'Cross-examined? Cross-examined? I've never heard of such a thing. I refuse to be cross-examined. My word should be good enough. Now I told you I could only see you for a few minutes. I'm very busy. Now, there's a good fellow, don't look so miserable. I know all about these actions. We'll win it all right. Just you go ahead. Do everything necessary. Get any counsel you like. And let me have the bill in due course. Brown won't pay your costs when you've won, I know. But I don't mind about that. I'm not going to be blackmailed. So don't you settle on any account. We'll fight the blackguard. You'll see. Now, run along, there's a good fellow.'

From time to time after that interview Mr Rounce tried to find out from a succession of Mr Bean's secretaries whether Mr Bean was prepared to give evidence or not. He sent him an extract from counsel's Opinion saying that without Mr Bean's evidence the plaintiff would be bound to succeed. He thought it more diplomatic at that stage not to send the remainder of the Opinion, which said that even if Mr Bean did give evidence it was most unlikely that the defence would succeed in view of the correspondence.

The substance of all this information Gilbert gathered from the file. Was it trivial or important? That was the question. He did not at that time know exactly how many actions for wrongful dismissal had been brought against Mr Bean or his Company, and, without that knowledge, it was difficult to make a decision. Eventually he made one, and went to see his employer.

'What do you want? The whole point of having a tame solicitor is to get time to do real work.'

'*Brown v Clarion Newspapers.* D'you want to give evidence?'

'That nonsense. I thought it was settled years ago. Is it still going on?'

'Yes, it's in the list tomorrow.'

'Well, tell them to settle. Anything else as you're here?'

'No, thank you, sir. I think it's a very sensible course. You'd have been bound to lose.'

'And who the hell asked for your opinion? It isn't even right. If I chose to give evidence, we'd win for certain. But I can't waste my time listening to counsel and judges talking all day. I'd get nothing else done. And I'd have you know, Swanley, that if I say an action will be won, it will be won. Wrongful dismissal or any other. What notice are you on anyway?'

CHAPTER TWO

Words Complained Of

At the time of the settlement of the action *Brown v Clarion Newspapers Ltd* (if payment by the defendants of the full amount of the claim and costs can fairly be termed a settlement), the train of events which led to the crime against a High Court judge was still a long way from the judge. It was, perhaps, not quite accurate to say that Gilbert's interview with Mr Bean was the earliest act to which the crime can be traced. Literally, one could trace it further back, for example to the first meeting of Gilbert's father and mother and the cause of it – to the first meeting of his grandmother and grandfather on each side of the family and to the causes for those meetings – indeed, with outside assistance, one could have gone right back to the Creation. Not a very profitable pursuit. So it is proposed to omit too remote and minor causes of the crime and to record only those important occurrences which ultimately led to it. The acceptance of his employment by Gilbert was the first of these. The action of *Brown v Clarion Newspapers Ltd* was the second. The third was the action of the Selection Committee in including in the team to play in the first Test Match against Australia, in the first year of Gilbert's employment by Clarion Newspapers Ltd, an amateur slow bowler called Lynsted and in omitting another amateur slow bowler called Rodmersham. Mr Bean was very fond of cricket. He both watched and played the game. He regularly arranged matches between the team of a village in the neighbourhood of one of his estates and a side of his own. On such occasions it was specially agreed that County players should strengthen the village team. A resolution was passed by the village cricket club to enable players who had no connection with the village to play for it. Mr Bean's team was always a very strong one. The game was played in perfect conditions when the weather was kind, and Mr Bean's hospitality to both teams was such that he had little difficulty in obtaining the services of any amateur and of any professional who was not bound by contract to play elsewhere. One of his favourites was Rodmersham. He was not only an extremely good slow bowler but he was a pleasant young man and knew how to flatter Mr Bean's vanity without overdoing it. He played for Mr Bean's team whenever he was wanted and introduced him to other cricket celebrities. In return, Mr Bean entertained him royally, and a house party in the summer at one of Mr Bean's houses was seldom without Philip Rodmersham.

Shortly before the Selection Committee announced the team, all the newspapers controlled by Mr Bean had been steadily pushing the claims of Philip Rodmersham and, indeed, there was a great deal to be said for his inclusion in the team. Even newspapers which Mr Bean did not control mentioned him as a likely candidate. Just before the team was announced he made a faultless fifty and took seven for forty-five against one of the stronger Counties. From Mr Bean's point of view Rodmersham's inclusion in the team was a foregone conclusion. It was, therefore, with anger and dismay that he found out that another first-class amateur, Lynsted, had been selected instead. There was not a great deal to choose between them, and the selection of either would have been perfectly justifiable, but Mr Bean considered it an outrage and, as his friendship with Rodmersham was well known, he took it as a personal affront to himself. He at once telephoned one of the most influential of the Selection Committee, Henry Gloster, whom he had met once or twice.

'This is Alexander Bean speaking. I've just seen the Test Team.'

'Oh, yes?'

'Why isn't Rodmersham in it?'

'I'm afraid I can't discuss that on the telephone.'

'I'll come round and see you then.'

'I'm afraid I can't discuss it at all.'

'Then why say you can't discuss it on the telephone?'

There was a pause.

'Well – why?' repeated Mr Bean.

'I'm sorry but we can't discuss these matters outside the Committee.'

'It's perfectly outrageous. Rodmersham was an obvious choice. Look at his performance against Yorkshire.'

'Yes – we bore that in mind.'

'Oh – you did, did you? And I suppose you also bore in mind that Lynsted is a personal friend of yours.'

'That's an outrageous suggestion.'

'Do you dispute that he is an intimate friend of yours?'

'I refuse to discuss the matter. Goodbye.'

'You shall hear more of this,' said Mr Bean, but Mr Gloster had already rung off.

The next morning the *London Clarion* carried on its sports page in banner headlines:

'SELECTION COMMITTEE CHOOSE ONE OF THEIR FRIENDS'

The article below said, among other things:

'We do not suggest that Max Lynsted is not a first-class cricketer. It may well be that he would, in due course, become a Test cricketer, but it is patently obvious to any follower of the game that his claims do not compare with those of Philip Rodmersham. Accordingly, Mr Alexander Bean thought it right to ask Mr Gloster why the surprising choice and omission had been made. MR GLOSTER DID NOT DISPUTE THAT MAX LYNSTED IS A CLOSE PERSONAL FRIEND OF HIS. Can that be the reason? We leave our readers to judge for themselves.'

This was too much for the Selection Committee, and the Chairman, Tom Bowgill, consulted solicitors on their behalf. Before any action could be taken, however, the *London Clarion* produced a further article in its next issue. Again there were banner headlines.

'SAVE ENGLAND FROM THEIR FRIENDS

Merit alone should be the selectors' guide. But has it been? In a conversation between Mr Gloster and Mr Bean the former implied that Max Lynsted had been chosen *because of his friendship with him* (the italics are ours). He did not say so in terms, but this was the only reasonable inference to be drawn from what he said. Although, no doubt, it would be hard on Lynsted, there is still time to make a change in the team. This journal believes that the selectors should make that change before the British public changes them.'

The following day Clarion Newspapers Ltd and Mr Bean each received a letter from the Committee's solicitors. It required an immediate withdrawal and apology, payment of damages to a charity, and an undertaking not to publish any similar statements. The *London Clarion* printed the letter in full, under banner headlines with the following comment:

'SELECTION COMMITTEE'S CRY FOR HELP

Today we received the following letter from the Committee's solicitors.'

Then followed the letter.

'It is a pity that the Committee seek help from the lawyers instead of helping themselves. The remedy is simple. Make Lynsted twelfth man and put Rodmersham in his place. This is cricket. What have lawyers to do with it? Solicitors are no doubt very good in their way, but they make bills of costs, not runs. They take your money, not wickets. This is our answer to the Committee. The game is cricket. The British public want the best team the country can produce. The Selection Committee have failed in their duty. While there is still time let them play the game and forget personal considerations. But if they insist on playing at the game of law, well, this journal can play at that too. But it will not be intimidated by solicitors' letters and it WILL NOT BE MUZZLED.'

The result of this second article was the immediate issue of a writ by the Committee's solicitors. Messrs Rounce and Ponsonby accepted service on behalf of the defendants and, at Mr Bean's request, Mr Rounce at once went down to see counsel. The barrister whom Messrs Rounce and Ponsonby normally employed was a middle-aged junior of the highest ability and integrity. But he had one thing in common with Mr Bean. He too was a megalomaniac, though it took a somewhat different form with him. Before Mr Rounce left for his first conference with Mr Gillingham, the barrister in question, he spoke to his secretary.

'Better not make any appointments for a couple of hours or so.'

'Will your conference with Mr Gillingham take all that long, sir?'

'It shouldn't, but it will. I shan't be allowed to say a word about the case for the first half-hour while he tells me about his latest achievements. The ingenuousness of the man is beyond belief. If he weren't pretty well the best junior at the Bar, we'd have given him up years ago. But he knows his stuff all right.'

Shortly afterwards Mr Rounce entered the chambers where Mr Gillingham practised, and was soon shown into the great man's room. He knew exactly what was coming. And it came.

'Come in, my dear Rounce. So very pleased I was able to see you. As a matter of fact, it's just a bit of luck that I could manage it. I had a consultation with the Attorney General about a most important matter. You'll probably read about it in the papers soon. But fortunately we've had to put it off until tomorrow.'

'It's very good of you to see me at such short notice.'

'Not at all, delighted. There's another bit of luck as it happens. I had a case in the House of Lords. I thought it would have gone on for some days. But it finished this morning. I was doing it on my own. And I soon saw I'd brought them round. They were dead against me when I started. Every one of them. Of course, it was rather a difficult point. We'd lost in the Court of Appeal. I hadn't been in the case then. Herbert Walter and Manton were doing it. As a matter of fact they advised the clients that there wasn't a chance. Luckily for them – though I say it myself – they came to me for an opinion. I read the papers and said they were right – dead right. But I had an awful tussle in the Lords, you know. But they came round in the end.'

'Did they congratulate you on your argument?' asked Mr Rounce, who, although he was used to all this, liked it less and less. He would not have dreamed of speaking like this to anyone else, but he knew that Mr Gillingham would be delighted. As indeed he was.

'Now, it's funny you should ask that,' he said. 'As a matter of fact, Lord Billiter did say he was very much indebted to me for my very great assistance to their Lordships.'

'That must have been very gratifying.'

'Well, I was quite pleased. After all, I'd put a lot of work into the case and it's nice to have one's efforts appreciated. Praise is sweet, you know. And one needs something to make up for all the labour,' – and Mr Gillingham pointed to the briefs on his table. All the important ones were turned round so that the visitor could see the fee marked and the names of the instructing solicitors. The small ones, or those from lesser known solicitors, were, strangely enough, facing Mr Gillingham.

'You see that brief,' went on Mr Gillingham, pointing to a large set of papers.

'I'd heard you were in that,' said Mr Rounce. 'A most interesting case.'

'Do you know the fee I'm getting? The brief's not marked yet, but it's been pretty well arranged by my Clerk. Ten thousand guineas.'

'Very handsome, but I expect you'll earn it.'

'As a matter of fact, I'm being led by George Huntingdon. His Clerk only wanted three thousand. But my Clerk insisted. "You'll have to ask fifteen," he said. "I'm not going to have Mr Gillingham going into Court in this case for less than ten thousand." "But the leader on the other side has only got five." "That's exactly what I mean," said my Clerk. "Mr Gillingham's worth two of him." A good chap, my Clerk. He knows his job all right. Been my Clerk ever since I came to the Bar.'

'You don't say?'

'Yes, indeed. I remember the first briefs I used to get. Delighted to go to an inquest for a couple of guineas. But, even then, you know, the writing was on the wall. I remember the first case I ever had as a matter of fact. In a County Court. D'you know, I didn't feel nervous at all. I just told the judge what the law was – I soon found out that I knew more than he did – and made my submission on the facts. We ought really to have lost the case.'

'But you won, I expect?'

'Well – yes – we did. To tell you the truth, I was a bit surprised. I didn't think I should find it as easy as I did. But, of course, it was only a County Court.'

'I don't suppose you went to the County Court for long?'

'Well – for about a couple of years, you know. As a matter of fact I did find it very useful. A good place to learn. But, after I got a High Court practice, I couldn't manage the travelling.'

'Of course not.'

'For a time my Clerk let me go provided the brief was marked not less than fifty guineas. But there weren't many cases which could stand such a fee. It meant the client losing money even though he won the case. That happens too often as it is. Too many Pyrrhic victories at law. I don't know what can be done about it. But I meant to tell you what the County Court judge said in my first case. He asked me and my opponent to tea after it was over. I told him it was my first case and d'you know what he said?'

'Please tell me,' said Mr Rounce, not even trying to say it in a tone which indicated that he wanted to hear. He knew that he would be told anyway and that Mr Gillingham, when in that particular mood, was incapable of noticing any inflexion in the voice. It was extraordinary that a man of such ability and intelligence should have had this astonishing kink.

'Well,' said Mr Gillingham, 'I remember it as clearly as if it were taking place now. "I don't think we've met before, Gillingham?" the judge said. "How long have you been called?" "Since yesterday, Judge," I said. "Bless my soul," said the judge, "you can't mean it." "I do, Judge, really," I said. "Well, it's the most astonishing performance I've ever seen or heard of," he said. "Knocks FE into a cocked hat." '

'Remarkable,' said Mr Rounce, and he meant it.

After another quarter of an hour of reminiscences and self-appreciation Mr Gillingham said it was about time they discussed the matter in hand. Stifling a sigh of relief, Mr Rounce told him. Mr Gillingham's manner immediately changed, and he began to speak as a normal individual again. Indeed, he even listened and only interrupted with intelligent queries.

'What Mr Bean wants to know,' said Mr Rounce, 'is whether he can go on publishing similar articles until the trial.'

'You say he's going to justify?' By justification is meant the assertion of the truth of the words complained of. The Committee were alleging that the words published by the *London Clarion* meant that they had chosen Lynsted not of merit but simply because he was a friend of one of their number, and that they were not fit to be Test Selectors. Mr Bean desired to defend the action on the ground that this was in fact the truth.

'Yes,' said Mr Rounce. 'He's quite determined to do so, and he said that, if he justified, the plaintiffs couldn't stop him publishing the same kind of statements.'

'That's true up to a point,' said Mr Gillingham. 'This application for an interim injunction will fail if we're justifying. But Mr Bean mustn't forget about Contempt of Court. This action will be tried by a jury probably, and, if he goes on publishing this kind of statement, it might prejudice the fair trial of the action. I think he can safely publish one more, if I see it first, but then it'll have to stop until after the trial.'

'I see,' said Mr Rounce. 'He won't like that.'

'I dare say he won't, but, unless he wants to end up in prison, he'll have to like it. And there's another thing. I've had a number of actions for Mr Bean or some of his companies in the past. And so have other people in the Temple. He moves about a bit.'

'Not since he came to you.'

'Well, he may have to move this time, unless he satisfies me that he really will give evidence. That man has never once been into the witness box, and I'm not going to put down a plea of justification unless I'm assured that he really will give evidence this time. There must be no doubt about it. And I want a written statement, signed by him, that he'll do it. Otherwise I won't plead justification. It's a very grave libel, and it isn't fair to put pleas like that on the record if the man who makes the statement won't face cross-examination. At any rate, I won't do it. So that's the first thing. Either I have his assurance or he can start moving round the Temple again.'

'Would it do if he gave it to you in person? I think he might be rather offended at my insisting on a promise in writing.'

'Oh yes, that would be perfectly all right.'

In consequence of this interview, a conference was arranged so that the great men could meet. There was certainly a clash of personalities at the beginning. Mr Bean opened the proceedings with: 'Well, Mr Gillingham, what can I do for you? I can't stay long, I'm afraid. As you probably know, my newspapers occupy most of my time.'

'Quite so, Mr Bean,' said Mr Gillingham genially. 'I'm very glad I was able to see you. As a matter of fact, I nearly had to cancel the appointment. I'm acting for the Prime Minister and he wanted to come to see me. Fortunately, however, I was able to give him an alternative appointment.'

'Most fortunate,' commented Mr Bean. 'Otherwise it would have meant that my changing the time of my meeting with the Governor of the Bank of England would have been to no purpose.'

'I act for the Bank of England in a number of its affairs, as a matter of fact. That brief over there, I think – ' Mr Gillingham paused and picked up a brief. 'Oh, no, that's the Bank of France. I've let my Opinion in the Bank of England go out already. I'd forgotten. It's difficult to keep pace with all one's work.'

'If I didn't keep a personal eye on my newspapers,' said Mr Bean, 'they wouldn't have the circulation they now enjoy. I'm afraid that unless we can get down to business I shall have to go back to my office with one of us dissatisfied.'

'I'm so sorry,' said Mr Gillingham, even more genially. 'I didn't realise you were in such a hurry. I find that the best way of doing my work is not to hurry about it. I think I should die of nervous exhaustion if I didn't let up between cases. You've no idea of the hours I put in every day.'

'Well – Mr Gillingham – what do you want to put into this half-hour?'

Mr Gillingham resigned himself to discussing the case against *Clarion Newspapers*.

'I just want to be satisfied, before I settle your defence in this action, that you are definitely going to give evidence.'

'Of course I'll give evidence.'

'You'll understand, Mr Bean, that I have a certain responsibility as counsel. I have a duty to the Court, the Bar and the public, as well as to my client.'

'I am well aware of the duties of a barrister. I read for the Bar myself.'

'Then you will understand that I will only make grave allegations against other people if I am satisfied that there is reasonable ground for making them and that my clients have reasonable evidence to justify the making of them.'

'You have my evidence.'

'Would you mind repeating to me what Mr Gloster said to you?'

'He admitted that the place had been given to Lynsted because he was a friend of his.'

'That's an extraordinary admission to make.'

'It's an extraordinary thing to do.'

'I agree, but I cannot conceive how a man who was guilty of such behaviour could admit it.'

'He lost his temper. What he said was: "All right, I agree; what the hell are you going to do about it?" '

'What had you said to which he was agreeing?'

'I had accused him of giving the place to Lynsted because he was a friend of his. At first he denied it. But, after a little more conversation, he admitted it. The actual words I can't remember exactly, but it's quite definite that he made the admission.'

'All right, Mr Bean, I've seen your proof of evidence to the effect you've mentioned, and, if you assure me you'll give evidence, I'll plead justification.'

'I have already assured you.'

'Very well then. I ought to add, however, that you will almost certainly lose the action.'

'I thought that would be for the jury to say.'

'I'm telling you what, in all probability, they will say before you spend a great deal of money in the hope that they won't.'

'You will allow me to have my own views on this matter. We shall win this action. I hope you'll remember this conversation when we do.'

'I certainly shall, when I've recovered from the shock. Seriously, Mr Bean, on what you tell me you are entitled to have this defence put forward, if you insist, but I should not be discharging my duty to you if I did not warn you that it's as hopeless as any case can be, particularly in view of the different version you've already given in the *Clarion*. I've a pretty wide and long experience of these matters and I do know what I'm talking about.'

'I don't doubt it, Mr Gillingham. I don't doubt that you think we'll lose. But just you wait and see. You'll get the surprise of your life. You've never seen me in the witness box before.'

Mr Gillingham refrained from saying that no one else had either. The conference ended and Mr Gillingham, having done his duty, settled a defence for his clients. The essential paragraph read as follows:

'The words complained of with and further or alternatively without the meanings alleged are true in substance and in fact.'

Back at his office Mr Bean sent for Gilbert.

'Oh, Swanley, this cricket party action. There's no hurry about it.'

'Yes, sir?'

'When Rounce and Ponsonby ask you for anything, don't be too quick to give it to them.'

'Very good, sir. May I know the reason?'

'I'm in no particular hurry for the action to come on. I've got some real work to do. I don't want to be tied down to days in Court.'

'I see, sir. I gather that you're going to give evidence yourself?'

'So I have told Mr Gillingham in person.'

'What does he think of our chances?'

'Nothing at all. These lawyers are always the same. If he said we'd a good case and we lost it, he thinks we'd be disappointed. If he says we've a bad case, it's a feather in his cap if he wins and "I told you so" available in large letters if we lose. That's all, Swanley. Nothing you want of me?'

'No, thank you, sir,' said Gilbert.

'Well, don't stand there looking like that. I can read your thoughts. They're wrong, as usual. You and I will fall out if you don't think on the right lines.'

Gilbert controlled himself and left his employer, but he confided to Alice that night (they were now happily married) that he wasn't sure how much longer he would last.

'Oh, do try to stay there till we've got young Gilbert fairly launched – till he can walk, anyway.'

Gilbert looked fondly at his wife.

'All right,' he said. 'If you'll promise me a Gilbert, I'll try and keep it up till then.'

CHAPTER THREE

Full Report of the Game

Every day during term one of the judges in the Queen's Bench Division deals with applications for adjournments of cases. Such applications are made on a variety of grounds, illness or absence abroad of the parties or their witnesses, late disclosure of documents, engagement of counsel in the House of Lords in another case, and a number of other reasons which are often rightly interpreted by the judge as a failure by one side or the other or both to be ready for the trial. Some judges take the view that, if the solicitors have not prepared their cases in time, that is just too bad and the case must come on for trial nevertheless, unsatisfactorily prepared. The solicitors will perhaps be more careful another time, such judges think. Other judges think that the important thing is that litigants should feel at the end of a case that they have had a fair hearing and that, as far as possible, everything has been done to present their cases properly to the Court. These judges grant adjournments even if the failure to have the case ready is simply due to the carelessness of one or other or both solicitors. They have the power to order solicitors to pay for their carelessness, and the exercise of that power from time to time, one would have thought, would have been quite sufficient to prevent the lists from getting into disorder owing to too many applications for adjournments. After all, the Courts are Courts of Justice, and though, of course, any man-made system of justice must go wrong from time to time, there seems no very good reason for compelling parties to fight their cases when they are not ready to do so. This is hardly likely to arrive at justice or an appearance of justice. To keep the lawyers in order, but, as far as possible, to see that the parties have no good reason for being dissatisfied with the trial of their cases, would appear to be a sound course for a judge to take. But Mr Justice Burpham did not think on these lines, and it was almost useless to apply to him for an adjournment of a case on the ground that the parties were not ready for trial. Indeed, except upon medical grounds, it was difficult to obtain an adjournment from him at all. His reputation was well known among both branches of the legal profession.

One day, when the case of *Bowgill and Others v Clarion Newspapers Ltd* was getting near to the top of the list and likely to be coming on for trial in about a fortnight, Mr Bean sent for Gilbert.

'Tell Rounce and Ponsonby,' he said, 'to apply for an adjournment in the Bowgill case.'

Gilbert happened to know that Mr Justice Burpham was at that time in charge of the list in which the case appeared.

'On what grounds, sir?' he asked. 'It'll be pretty difficult to get an adjournment. Burpham's in charge of the list.'

'I don't care in the least who's in charge of the list. It's not convenient for me for the case to come on at present. Get an adjournment for a couple of months or so.'

'We can ask for one, but we won't get it.'

'Don't stand there arguing, Swanley. Get on with it.'

In due course, Mr Gillingham applied to Mr Justice Burpham for an adjournment.

'On what grounds?' asked the judge. Mr Gillingham told him as best he could.

'This application is dismissed with costs,' said the judge. Gilbert was surprised to find that Mr Bean was not in the least put out by the news.

'Apply again next week,' were his orders. 'There may be a different judge in charge of the list.' There was, in fact, a different judge, but the grounds of the application were so flimsy that that application, too, was dismissed with costs. Again Mr Bean did not appear disturbed.

'Very well,' he said, 'we must get on with it.'

Eventually the day of the trial arrived. It was a popular sporting event, and, as there was nothing spectacular in the news at the time, the press prepared to make the most of it. The members of the Selection Committee were represented by Sir Giles Farnaby, QC, the ex-Attorney-General, and Mr John Cloncarrig. The defendants, Mr Bean and Clarion Newspapers Ltd, were represented by Mr Augustus Cramp, QC, and Mr Gillingham. The judge was Mr Justice Broad. He sat with a jury.

One of the newspapers sent a famous cricket correspondent – Andrew Spottiswoode – to report the case, and his version of the proceedings started like this: 'It was a perfect day when the umpires – who in this somewhat unusual match consisted of Mr Justice Broad and nine good men and true and three good women and true (one of them rather attractive) – took up their appointed positions. The bowling was opened from the plaintiffs' end by John Cloncarrig, but he obviously made no impression whatever and he was soon replaced by Giles Farnaby. He kept a very good length. His first over went something like this: "May it please your Lordship, members of the jury, as you have just heard from my learned friend, this is a claim for damages for libel and it is brought by the plaintiffs in circumstances which you may think have never been paralleled. The plaintiffs are all cricketers of distinction who act as the Committee which selects the team for England against Australia. Everyone recognises that the Committee is not infallible. Some of you may, for example, think that certain cricketers who have been chosen to represent England should not have been included in the team and that others who have been left out of the team should have been included. You are, of course, entitled to say so. So are the defendants. So is everyone. But the allegation which has been made by the defendants in this case is that the selection of one member of the team has been made in bad faith, that it has been made not on merit but solely for reasons of personal friendship. In other words, it is alleged that the Committee has acted corruptly. It would be just as bad if it were alleged that they had taken money for selecting a particular cricketer. It is an allegation of the utmost gravity, and, although in the past there has often been controversy – even heated controversy – as far as my memory serves me such a suggestion has never been made before. You may well think, therefore, that the whole honour of British cricket is at stake, and that no other course was open to the plaintiffs but to bring this action to vindicate that honour and themselves." '

The report went on:

'Sir Giles bowled several more overs of the same calibre and then, to my surprise, he took himself off and put on John Cloncarrig again. The odd thing about this particular game was that members of the same side seemed to be bowling at each other. For example, Cloncarrig started bowling to the Chairman of the Committee, Tom Bowgill. Needless to say, Bowgill had no difficulty whatever in dealing with his deliveries. Indeed, it was obvious to the crowded Court that Cloncarrig was sending down just the sort of ball which Bowgill liked. Perhaps the promoters of brighter cricket could learn something from this. However, after a few overs of easy stuff from Cloncarrig, Augustus Cramp came on at the defendants' end. It was soon quite plain that this was bowling of quite a different order. His first ball looked innocent enough, but Tom Bowgill played it with great respect.

' "I'm afraid I shall have to ask you a little about the secrets of the Committee room, Mr Bowgill. I hope you won't mind."

' "I shall answer any questions which his Lordship says I must."

'The next ball was fast and straight and Tom Bowgill simply blocked it.

' "Would you mind telling me in detail exactly what material the Committee has in front of it when it selects a team?"

' "In detail?"

'The third ball was bowled at once.

' "Yes, if you please."

'Tom Bowgill blocked it again.

' "That will take a very long time."

'But Augustus Cramp continued to bowl straight at the wicket and Tom Bowgill was forced to play him. Every now and then a ball was slightly off the stumps and usually at first Tom would then leave it. He was not going to risk a catch. But, as the bowling went on, Tom became a little bolder. He started scoring singles. His first boundary came after twenty minutes. The question was:

"Mr Bowgill, when you are considering what selections to make, do you pay any attention to the opinions of cricketing journalists which you may have read?" The reply was: "Oh, yes –." There was a pause and the witness went on, "for what they are worth." What one might call a late cut.'

Mr Spottiswoode's report continued in the same strain. The plaintiffs had obviously determined to crush the defendants. Every member of the selection committee was called to give evidence. The most important witness was, of course, Henry Gloster. Although it appeared obvious to everyone that he had acted in good faith, he was nevertheless rather nervous in the witness box, as many witnesses, unused to giving evidence at all, let alone in such a crowded court, often are. In the words of Mr Spottiswoode:

'Then came a difficult ball, which Henry Gloster did not seem quite to know what to do with. The question was: "I imagine that you were pleased to be able to offer the place to Max Lynsted as he is such a close personal friend of yours?" His answer was: "I haven't said he was a close personal friend."

'Augustus Cramp immediately appealed to the judge.

' "His actual words, Mr Cramp, were: 'Yes, certainly, he's a friend of mine. I've known him for years.' "

'The next ball was an extremely difficult one to play, and Mr Gloster was nearly bowled.

' "Do you desire to distinguish between a close personal friend and a person who is certainly a friend whom you've known for years?"

' "I'm not trying to distinguish anything."

'This answer resulted in something which the brighter cricket advocates should also consider, because the umpire himself, Mr Justice Broad, immediately sent one down to Mr Gloster. It was very fast and might fairly have been described as a bumper. It nearly laid the batsman out.

' "Now, Mr Gloster, don't prevaricate. You know perfectly well what is meant by a close personal friend or an intimate friend. Was Mr Lynsted in that category?"

' "Yes, my Lord."

' "Very well, then. Don't let's have any more nonsense about not trying to distinguish anything."

'Henry Gloster (metaphorically) rubbed his knuckles. He did not relish the judge's bowling and was quite relieved when Augustus Cramp came on again.'

The plaintiffs' case continued, each of them was examined and cross-examined until, in the words of Mr Spottiswoode: 'The plaintiffs eventually closed their innings after having put up quite a useful score. It remains to be seen what reply the defendants can make.'

The case had now taken two days, but Mr Bean had not been present on either of them. He had told Gilbert to assure Rounce and Ponsonby that he would be available when he was wanted and would come at any time on half an hour's notice. To his counsel's request that he should be present at any rate during the evidence of Henry Gloster, he had replied by saying that he didn't keep a dog and bark himself. On the Tuesday evening he was informed that he would be required at 10.30 on the following day. Wednesday morning arrived, the Court was crowded and everyone was waiting for Mr Bean to go into the witness box. At 10.15 he had not arrived and Mr Rounce began to become anxious. At 10.25 there was still no Mr Bean, and, although Mr Rounce knew that the case would first be opened to the jury by Augustus Cramp, who could spin it out if necessary, he became extremely worried. Just before 10.30 a special messenger arrived with a note. It contained a doctor's certificate saying that Mr Bean was unable to give evidence as he was confined to bed in a nursing home, suffering from an acute anxiety state. The certificate was signed by a West End psychiatrist. With the certificate was a note scribbled by Mr Bean. It simply said: 'Apply for adjournment. AB.' Mr Rounce only had time to say: 'This is a nice kettle of fish,' and to hand the note and certificate to Mr Cramp before the judge came in.

'My Lord,' said Mr Cramp, 'I have just this moment been handed a medical certificate which says in effect that the chief witness for the defence is unable to give evidence. I have not had time to tell my learned friend.'

'Let me see the certificate,' said Mr Justice Broad. 'Humph!' he commented. 'A lot of people get anxious when litigation is pending. Well, what do you say, Sir Giles?'

'I certainly can't consent to an adjournment, my Lord. With respect, in my submission the doctor who gave this certificate should be present to be cross-examined. There has been no suggestion of any ill-health by Mr Bean up till this moment. It is an extraordinary coincidence that he should be taken ill – with an illness of this kind – just at the precise moment he is required to give evidence, particularly as two applications for adjournments of the trial, made on totally different grounds, have been refused in the last three weeks.'

'I think the less said about the matter at the moment the better,' said the judge. 'I am certainly not prepared to grant an adjournment at this stage on this evidence, but I shall give you an opportunity of renewing your application if you call the doctor who gave this certificate. Meantime, you can open the case to the jury.'

'Would your Lordship forgive me if I had a word with my learned junior?'

'Certainly, Mr Cramp.'

The two counsel conferred for a few moments. Then: 'My Lord,' said Mr Cramp, 'while I fully appreciate what your Lordship has said, I do not see how I can properly comply with your Lordship's direction. The defence in this action is justification. To succeed in that defence I must be in a position to call Mr Bean. It would not be right for me to address the jury without knowing whether I shall be in a position to call my essential witness. Should your Lordship refuse an adjournment, it is plain that that witness will not be available. In his absence, it would not, in my view, be right for me to make any submissions to the jury. Accordingly, I can only ask your Lordship for a short adjournment in order to try to bring the doctor here to give evidence about the state of Mr Bean's health.'

'I see your difficulty,' said the judge. 'It is extremely inconvenient for everyone, but I think that is the only course to take. Your clients must get into touch with the doctor at once and let me know the result. Meantime, I will rise and go to my room. The jury had better remain in their places until you can give me some news as to how long it will take to bring the doctor here.'

During the three weeks which preceded the trial of the action Mr Bean had (unknown to Gilbert or any of his employees) been regularly visiting the psychiatrist in question, Dr McLong. At the first consultation, after Mr Bean had introduced himself, the conversation proceeded as follows: 'Dr McLong, I'm in rather a bad way. I hope you'll be able to help me.'

'Sit down and relax, Mr Bean. I'll do what I can.'

'It is vitally important that no one should know how ill I really am. It would have the gravest effect upon my newspapers.'

'Naturally your visits are absolutely confidential. What is the trouble?'

'Everything. No one who meets me during the day would have the slightest idea that there was anything wrong with me. They would be quite amazed.'

'Tell me the symptoms.'

'Physically I'm well enough.'

'I imagined that was the case. Take your time. Tell me the worst symptoms.'

'It's so difficult to know the worst, there are so many. As a matter of fact, I know a certain amount about medicine and psychiatry myself. So I'm able to look at myself quite objectively and I realise that it's absolute nonsense for me to have any of these symptoms at all. I tell myself that every time they occur. But it just makes no difference. I've tried hard to overcome it by myself. I know that's the best way. But I just haven't been able to do so. I'm at the end of my tether and so I've come to you.'

'Very sensible of you to come for advice. Go on.'

'I suffer from claustrophobia, agoraphobia and insomnia. If I'm in a car I want to stop it and get out. When I get out, I want to get in again. If I eat something, I suddenly wish I hadn't and almost faint from the frustration of not being able to be in the position of not having eaten it.'

'Well-known symptoms, Mr Bean. Anything else?'

'The same kind of thing in every direction. If I'm in London, I want to be in the country and vice versa. I want to be able to go everywhere at the same time and suffer agonies from the frustration of not being able to do it.'

'Well, Mr Bean, I think we can put you all right, but only if you'll trust me. It'll take time, but I can do it.'

'What will the treatment consist of?'

'I hope in just talking to me.'

'You say "you hope" – what does that imply?'

'Well – if necessary, you should go into a nursing home and have complete rest.'

'I can't do that. I have my work.'

'I dare say. We all say that. I'm hopelessly overworked myself.'

This was quite true. Ninety-nine per cent of his patients were women who enjoyed pouring out their innermost souls to him. He was overwhelmed with patients. He was good-looking, charged high fees, and listened sympathetically. He certainly did good to his patients. After a chat with him for an hour, or even half an hour, most of them went away with a feeling of well-being which other people only acquire by taking benzedrine or some similar drug. Once the barriers of convention have been overcome, it is delicious to most women – and some men – to speak frankly to a comparative stranger about their most intimate thoughts and actions. Dr McLong needed a rest himself and he certainly could afford it. 'Yes,' he went on, 'I may have to take a holiday myself. No one's indispensable.'

'I am,' said Mr Bean.

'You'll die one day, you know.'

'Of course. I accept that. I've made the necessary arrangements.'

'Suppose it were tomorrow?'

'It won't be. My physical health is good.'

'You might be run over.'

'It takes two to make an accident and I shan't be one of them.'

'There might be a war.'

'There won't be. Alarms and excursions, perhaps, but no war.'

'I haven't noticed the *London Clarion* preaching disarmament.'

'Of course not. If it did, there might be a war.'

'Well, Mr Bean, I see you're quite determined to live – which is an excellent thing. But if you don't respond sufficiently to treatment, you'll have to do what I say and take a rest.'

'Well – we'll wait and see if the need arises.'

'That's right.'

'When can I start the treatment?'

'Now – if you've time.'

'Half an hour any good to you?'

'Certainly. Perhaps you'd come and lie down over here. That's right. Now, just relax, and try to answer my questions truthfully. I shall know if you're not, you know, if that's any encouragement.'

Dr McLong then proceeded to psycho-analyse Mr Bean. He had seldom had a more co-operative patient. He appeared to have no inhibitions at all and he answered all the questions which at first on such occasions tend to embarrass, not only with frankness but with accuracy. The interview closed with satisfaction on both sides.

'That was excellent,' said Dr McLong. 'I've seldom had such a successful first treatment.'

'I'm very pleased you're satisfied,' said Mr Bean. These interviews had gone on during the three weeks, but, although Mr Bean continued to answer frankly and accurately nearly all the questions he was asked (though he threw in an occasional lie when he did not desire Dr McLong to know the truth) his symptoms, so far from yielding to the treatment, seemed to get worse.

'I was at Holborn this morning,' said Mr Bean, shortly before the trial had started, 'and I nearly fainted because I wasn't at Ludgate Circus.'

'Dear, dear,' said Dr McLong, 'that's bad. I must say, I'm surprised. It looks to me as though we shall need this rest.'

'But I've got this action coming on. I must be available to give evidence.'

'You can't give evidence if you've fainted at Holborn. Just suppose when you were in the witness box you suddenly wished you were somewhere else – that does happen, I believe, sometimes – you might faint in the box. That wouldn't do you or anyone else any good. No, Mr Bean, you're one of the most important men in the country, but, on this occasion, you really must be guided by me.'

Eventually, after some persuasion, Mr Bean allowed himself to be put into an extremely expensive nursing home. He actually went in on the day he was supposed to give evidence and, as soon as he was in bed, he had the doctor's certificate sent down to the Court.

Not long after Mr Justice Broad had adjourned to see if Dr McLong could be found, the psychiatrist's secretary informed him that solicitors were on the telephone asking for his attendance in Queen's Bench Court 4.

'I will be there in half an hour,' he said, but on the way he called on Mr Bean, and told him what was happening.

'But, Doctor,' said Mr Bean, 'you're not going to answer questions about my symptoms. They were told you in complete confidence and I shall be ruined if the world knows about them.'

'It's a difficult problem,' said Dr McLong. 'There's no legal privilege given to a doctor.'

'You must refuse. You promised.'

'If I refuse to answer questions I'll be sent to gaol.'

'Well – go to gaol then. You said you wanted a rest. Make a test case of it. Should a doctor tell? I'll back you with all my newspapers. I'll pay you £5,000. It'll be free of tax.'

'Are you sure of that?' asked Dr McLong, who paid surtax with pain and regularity.

'Certainly. It'll be a windfall. Get your wife to send you in champagne and oysters. Prisoners in contempt can have their own food. It'll be a rest and a new experience and you will be a martyr to the cause so dear to the medical profession.'

'I won't promise,' said Dr McLong, 'but I will promise to do my best not to state your symptoms and I may – I may – if the worst comes to the worst, do what you suggest – on the terms you mention – of course.'

'I'll give you a cheque now if you like. Only to be cashed, of course, if you go to prison.'

'Oh – that's quite unnecessary really – but perhaps it might be the most sensible course.'

Shortly afterwards Dr McLong arrived at the Law Courts and Mr Justice Broad returned to Court. The psychiatrist at once went into the witness box. After giving evidence that he had been treating Mr Bean throughout the preceding three weeks and that in his view he was unfit to give evidence that day and might be unfit for some little time, he was cross-examined by Sir Giles Farnaby.

'What were Mr Bean's symptoms when he first consulted you?'

'Before answering that question, may I ask your Lordship's directions in the matter?'

'What direction do you want?' asked the judge.

'Whether I must answer the question, my Lord. These are confidential matters.'

'I quite understand that, Dr McLong, but I'm afraid you must answer. There is no privilege between doctor and patient in law.'

'May I say something about that, my Lord?'

'What is it you want to say? You have to answer the question.'

'But, my Lord, supposing I were treating a patient for kleptomania – '

'For what?' interrupted the judge.

'For kleptomania, my Lord.'

'I prefer to call it stealing,' said the judge.

'It is quite different from stealing, my Lord. It's a disease of the mind.'

'I hear you say so. I still prefer to call it stealing. As far as my experience goes, it only occurs after a person has been caught looting one of the big stores or the like.'

'I mustn't argue with your Lordship, but it is a disease recognised by the medical profession.'

'I suppose all crimes will soon be given medical names. What is the present word for robbery with violence or arson?'

The witness remained silent.

'Never mind,' said the judge. 'It will come in a few years. It will certainly be a help to those responsible for the country's prisons. They are hopelessly overcrowded at the moment. If the medical profession can persuade the public that thugs and tricksters require doses of some new drug and a comfortable stay in a country house which the owner can no longer afford to keep up, instead of good strong doses of imprisonment, the overcrowding problem will be solved anyway. Now – don't let's waste any more time. You must answer the question, Doctor.'

'But, my Lord, if I treat a patient – say for kleptomania – I often effect a cure and the result is a useful, or at any rate a safe, citizen instead of a dangerous one. But, in order to effect a cure, I have to obtain complete frankness from my patient and to induce him to tell me everything he has done. How can a patient be expected to do that if he knows that at any moment I may be compelled to state exactly what he has told me?'

'I don't know what this has got to do with the matter. You are not, I gather, treating Mr Bean for kleptomania or is that one of his symptoms?'

'Oh, no, my Lord, nothing of the kind.'

'I'm glad to hear it. Now, will you be good enough to answer counsel's question. I expect you've forgotten it by now. Would you repeat it, please, Sir Giles?'

'What were Mr Bean's symptoms when he first consulted you?'

There was no answer.

'Come along now, Doctor, your patient can have no complaint against you. I am telling you to answer. It is the law which is responsible.'

'I still feel I cannot break so serious a confidence, my Lord. Would your Lordship give me an opportunity of consulting some leading members of the medical profession? I would have done so before I came to Court, but, as your Lordship knows, I had no notice that I should be required and I came straight away.'

'No – I'm sorry, Doctor. You must answer the question.'

There was still no answer.

'Now – really, Doctor, we've wasted enough time over this matter already. You are going to be compelled to answer the question. There is no point in beating about the bush.'

'Unless perhaps, my Lord, there were no symptoms, when Mr Bean consulted him,' put in Sir Giles Farnaby helpfully.

'He certainly had symptoms – very definite symptoms, but, without intending the least disrespect to your Lordship or this Court, I cannot bring myself to state them without the patient's permission.'

'Can you obtain his permission then?'

'I'm afraid not. I tried before I came here, my Lord.'

'This is past a joke, Mr Cramp. Your client asks for an adjournment and then refuses to allow his doctor to disclose the symptoms of his illness – if any.'

'Psychiatrists would be out of business, my Lord, if patients could not rely on their statements being treated in confidence, my Lord.'

'Well,' said the judge, 'without wanting to be offensive to you, Dr McLong, I'm not sure that that would be entirely a bad thing.'

'You will forgive me for disagreeing, my Lord,' said Dr McLong.

'Certainly,' said the judge, 'but I will not forgive you for not answering the question. I'm afraid my patience is running out. I'm sorry to have to say this but, unless you decide to answer the question, I shall have to give you into the custody of the tipstaff and send you to prison for contempt of court. I don't want to have to do that, I assure you.'

Dr McLong hesitated. He thought of the cheque in his pocket, of the sensation his imprisonment would cause, of the possible results of that imprisonment, and of the fact that admittedly he could do with a rest himself.

'Well?' said the judge.

'I'm afraid I must place myself in your Lordship's hands. I am not prepared to answer the question.'

'Very well,' said the judge, 'if that's your answer, I have no alternative. Let the tipstaff take the witness into custody.'

Shortly afterwards, Dr McLong was removed to await transport to Brixton prison. Meantime, Mr Cramp renewed his application for an adjournment.

'I take it, Sir Giles,' said the judge, 'that you still object.'

'Most definitely, my Lord.'

'Very well, then. The application is refused. Without intending any criticism of Dr McLong, I am not satisfied of the bona fides of the application so far as the defendant Mr Bean is concerned. Now. Mr Cramp, you must address the jury on the basis that you will not be able to call Mr Bean.'

'My Lord,' said Mr Cramp, 'as I indicated before, I do not think I should be justified in so doing. It seems to me that if I am not to be given the opportunity of calling the chief witness for the defence, who is sworn by a qualified medical practitioner to be ill, there is no further assistance which either I or my learned junior can render to your Lordship or the jury or the defendants and we propose to retire from the case. Before doing so, I must ask your Lordship for leave to appeal against your Lordship's refusal to grant an adjournment.'

'Certainly not,' said the judge, 'you must go to the Court of Appeal for that if you think proper.'

'If your Lordship pleases. Before leaving the Court, I should like to assure your Lordship that neither I nor my learned junior intend the least disrespect to your Lordship, but we consider that the only proper course we can take is to withdraw.'

'Very well, Mr Cramp. No doubt you know what you are doing.'

The trial then proceeded. In the words of Mr Spottiswoode: 'Mr Cramp's action can hardly be compared to declaring an innings closed, though that is what it looked like at first. But that is only done when the declaring side has put up some kind of a score. In the case of the defendants, the score was 0 for 0, last player 0. But, although you might have expected the abandonment of the game by the defendants to result in the umpires drawing the stumps and the plaintiffs walking off victors by default, nothing of the kind happened. On the contrary, the game continued, and Sir Giles continued to bowl hard and accurately at no one. When he had finished, the judge proceeded to follow his example. One of his overs went like this: "Members of the jury, the only question you now have to consider is what damages should be paid to the plaintiffs. The only defence is that of justification and the burden of proving that lies on the defendants. As their counsel have withdrawn from the case and no evidence has been called on their behalf, the plaintiffs are entitled to a verdict at your hands. How much you award is entirely a matter for you, but you may think that the libel is a very grave one and that it has been made worse by the defendants putting on the record this plea of justification and then failing to call any evidence to establish it." '

After the judge had finished, the other umpires – the jury – retired. After half an hour they returned and signalled £5,000 to the scorer.

A full report of the proceedings appeared in all the newspapers including the *London Clarion*. In a leading article in that newspaper, the following passage occurred:

'We naturally do not seek to criticise the action of Mr

Justice Broad in refusing an adjournment, but the fact remains that this journal was by that refusal prevented from putting forward its defence. That seems to us unfortunate. We have been condemned unheard. But we must accept that misfortune. It would not be the first time that a decision which was right in law may have caused injustice. A far more serious matter, however, than this journal's position is that of Dr McLong, now lodged in Brixton prison for sticking to his principles. No doubt with the law as it is at present, the learned judge was right, and, indeed, was bound to act as he did. But how long is it going to be before the law is changed? It is time that Parliament took a hand in the matter. Otherwise no patient of a doctor will ever be able to consult him with that freedom and frankness which is quite essential in many cases if treatment is to be satisfactory. Suppose, for example, the technical and scientific director of a large public company, whose services could not be satisfactorily replaced by another, were dying of cancer. The notification of that fact to the public might seriously affect the value of the shares. Such examples could be multiplied a hundredfold. How long is this to go on? And for how long was Dr McLong to languish in Brixton prison? These are questions to which the British public is entitled to expect an early and satisfactory answer.'

It was not only the *London Clarion* but the whole of the London press which proceeded to debate fiercely the action of Dr McLong. As Mr Bean had rightly anticipated, he soon became almost a public hero, and a petition for his immediate release was signed by many hundred thousand people. With regard to the verdict against Clarion Newspapers Ltd, although the circumstances of Mr Bean's illness seemed suspicious to some people, the majority felt that it was unsatisfactory that the case had not been fought to a finish and that the defendants had apparently been deprived of the opportunity of giving evidence. They did not know that Mr Bean never had the slightest intention of giving evidence. He had successfully smeared the names of the selectors, and, although they obtained their verdict, people as a whole did not feel that they had been properly vindicated. Mr Bean had successfully prevented them from having that opportunity. Mr Cramp and Mr Gillingham sought instructions from Mr Bean through Messrs Rounce and Ponsonby as to whether they should apply for leave to appeal to the Court of Appeal. They stated that, in their view, there was quite a reasonable possibility of the appeal succeeding, and a new trial being ordered. Mr Rounce was allowed to have an interview with Mr Bean at his nursing home and he conveyed this opinion of counsel to him.

'Appeal?' said Mr Bean. 'Dear me, no. Mr Justice Broad is a very good judge. He was quite right in the circumstances. It's the law which is at fault. I have no complaint at all. We have suffered an injustice but these things must always happen. However, justice can never be perfect. No, pay the damages and forget it.'

Subsequently Mr Bean sent for the editor of the *London Clarion* and gave him detailed instructions as to how to make the most of the medical aspect of the case. 'If you play your cards properly,' he said, 'you should send the circulation up by half a million. With old McLong in gaol the public will concentrate on the medical problem and the injustice to him. Any slight feeling against us for the libel – and, in the circumstances, there will be very little – will soon be swallowed up in the Should a Doctor Tell? campaign. It's the best stunt we've had for years.'

Mr Bean also sent for Gilbert. All he said to him was: 'So you thought we should lose the action, did you? Still think so?'

Then, as Gilbert went to go, he called him back. 'Oh – Swanley, see that something tempting, caviare, foie gras and so on, is sent in to Dr McLong each day.'

CHAPTER FOUR

Mr Bean Gives Evidence

Dr McLong was eventually released after three months. The case having been disposed of, the judge felt he was able to compromise in the matter and did not insist on an answer to the question. Three months in prison was a sufficient vindication of the rule of law in the judge's opinion. At about the same time Mr Bean was discharged from the nursing home, where he had gradually conducted more and more business from his room, until it had become less like a room in a nursing home than a branch office of Clarion Newspapers Ltd, with editors and other employees attending daily.

A debate was arranged in the House of Commons on the medical aspects of the cricket action, but, as a result of the divergent views expressed, the Government said that it was not prepared to introduce legislation to alter the law. By that time, however, the *London Clarion* had acquired its extra half million readers, and the affair was allowed to peter out. Meanwhile, at Clarion House, employees came and went. Some of their actions for wrongful dismissal were defended and some were not, but all of them were lost by the newspaper company and in none of them did Mr Bean give evidence. Just after the third anniversary of his appointment, Gilbert, who had been finding things more and more difficult and who was quite looking forward to the inevitable notice, received a summons to go to see Mr Bean.

'Swanley,' said Mr Bean, 'how much notice d'you think you are entitled to?'

'I should say six months.'

'We must agree to differ. I think a week is ample. Here it is. You needn't work out your week. Just disappear. You've outlived your usefulness and you don't speak to me with the respect to which I am entitled.'

'Am I discharged then, sir?'

'You are – with a week's notice.'

'Very well, then. You aren't entitled to respect. You're a vainglorious megalomaniac and an exhibitionist of a peculiarly unpleasant kind. As I'm sacked, I've the right of any citizen to say what I like to you.'

'Get out.'

'In a moment, when I've finished. You'll hear from my solicitors, but only with a writ, as there's no point in sending letters which are not answered or only receive a short, irrelevant and impudent reply. The only thing I shall regret is that I shan't have the pleasure of seeing you in the witness box.'

'But you will, Swanley, you will. I shall recount the whole of this conversation to the judge. It ought to help you a lot to get another job. Now, get out. Or I'll send for one of the heavy workers to put you out.'

In due course the inevitable writ was issued and Mr Bean at once asked for a conference with Mr Gillingham. It was arranged, and Mr Rounce and Mr Bean attended at his chambers. As soon as they were shown into his room, Mr Bean began: 'Good afternoon, Mr Gillingham. I am well aware that you act for the Prime Minister, the Governor of the Bank of England, the Bank of France ...'

Mr Rounce was horrified. He himself occasionally indulged in a little mild sarcasm at the expense of Mr Gillingham and it passed over his head, but this was too much of a good thing. They would be thrown out of the chambers and he would have to apologise for his client's behaviour. But nothing of the sort happened. As soon as Mr Bean had finished his list of names, Mr Gillingham said pleasantly: 'How clever of you to remember, but you've left out several, you know – the Coal Board, for example, the London Transport Executive and who else d'you think you've forgotten?'

Mr Bean himself was puzzled. He had intended to end his speech by saying that now he, Alexander Bean, wanted advice and had not a great deal of time to spare. Instead, he found himself indulging in a sort of duet with Mr Gillingham; there was one theme and there were no variations. After a quarter of an hour of this, Mr Gillingham eventually said: 'And, of course, Mr Alexander Bean.'

'Which reminds me,' said Mr Bean. 'I want some advice.'

And, before he could be interrupted, he went on to ask it. 'If I say to an employee "take a week's notice" and he says "I'll tell you what you can do with your week's notice" or words to that effect, can't I dismiss him on the spot without any notice at all?'

'Normally, yes,' replied Mr Gillingham.

'Suppose he were entitled to a month's notice and I only gave him a week's notice, would that make any difference?'

Mr Gillingham thought for a moment. 'I suppose he might say that that was a repudiation of the contract – but I'm not so sure, and, even then, he has to minimise his damage. In order to do that he ought to serve you for a week and he can't talk to you like that while in your service. Of course, whether he ought to stay in your service for the week depends on all the circumstances. It raises quite a nice little problem. I suppose, that, if you deliberately provoked an employee to abuse you by giving him far too little notice, and his language to you were no more than was justified by the occasion, you couldn't dismiss him for that. Is this your idea or did you learn it from someone, Mr Bean? It's rather good. You want to dismiss an employee on the spot, but you've no ground for doing so. He's entitled to, say, three months' notice. Call him in and give him a week's notice. Then, if he abuses you like a fishwife, sack him on the spot without any notice at all. Yes – I think that one will work. I suppose the difficulty would be to get him to abuse you sufficiently.'

'This one has said quite sufficient,' said Mr Bean, and he stated what Gilbert had called him.

'Yes, that should do very nicely,' said Mr Gillingham. 'Most amusing. I shall enjoy this case, but' – and his face fell – 'how are we going to prove it?'

'I shall give evidence,' said Mr Bean.

'Quite,' said Mr Gillingham, 'but was there no other witness to the conversation except you – in case you're unavoidably detained somewhere on the day of the trial or taken ill or something?'

'I shan't be taken ill or something. No, no one else was present. I shall give the evidence, Mr Gillingham. I'll teach Master Swanley a well-needed lesson. Pile up the costs, Mr Rounce. Make him feel it when he's lost. And then make him bankrupt. No "honour among solicitors" stuff, please. Bleed him white. I'll teach him to talk like that to me. Such a thing has never happened before. You think I'll win all right, Mr Gillingham?'

'I think you'll have a very good chance if you give evidence and your evidence is accepted. Of course, I can't tell what Swanley will say.'

'Oh – he'll be all right. He's a truthful devil. You wouldn't think he was a solicitor. Don't mind me, Mr Rounce. Nothing personal intended. Good – well, that's all, Mr Gillingham, thank you. We'll show Master Swanley who's an exhibitionist.'

Some months afterwards the action came on for trial and, to everyone's amazement, Mr Bean not only attended the trial from its outset but actually went into the witness box when his turn came. It caused quite a sensation. Mr Justice Beverley was the judge, and, as the name of Mr Bean was well known in the Law Courts as a great litigant who never gave evidence, he looked at the witness with some interest. Mr Bean returned the judge's gaze quite coolly. After he had been examined by his own counsel, he was cross-examined, and it was this cross-examination which was one of the final events which led to the attempted blackmail of Mr Justice Beverley. Counsel cross-examining Mr Bean was inclined to be brusque and slightly annoyed the witness, who started to give somewhat irritable and occasionally impudent answers. Finally he said: 'What an incredibly stupid question,' whereupon the judge intervened.

'Mr Bean, you will apologise for that remark.'

Mr Bean said nothing.

'Mr Bean, you will apologise for that remark at once.'

The judge waited for the apology to begin. Nothing happened.

'I shall not ask you again,' said the judge, quietly and calmly. 'Unless you apologise at once for your insolence, I shall send you to prison for disobeying my order.'

'I apologise,' said Mr Bean in a toneless voice.

'You will now continue your evidence. But let me say this first. You have been behaving in a most unsatisfactory manner for some time, and you must kindly understand that, however you may behave outside this Court, inside it you will behave properly. Is that understood?'

Mr Bean said nothing.

'Is that understood, Mr Bean?'

'Yes,' said Mr Bean.

Mr Gillingham thought he should take a hand. 'You should say "My Lord" when you address his Lordship,' he said.

'That's all right, thank you, Mr Gillingham,' said the judge.

'My Lord,' said Mr Bean tonelessly, rather like a small boy repeating a lesson. His cross-examination then continued, but, to Mr Gillingham's surprise, he either said everything the cross-examining counsel wanted him to say or tied himself into such knots that the unravelling of them appeared a most formidable task.

'Come, do yourself justice, Mr Bean,' said counsel. 'You can't really mean that?'

'Perhaps I don't.'

'Then why did you say it?'

'I've no idea.'

The truth of the matter was that Mr Bean was hardly listening. He was thinking of one thing and one thing only – the judge. No one could speak to him as the judge had spoken without living to regret it. For part of his stay in the witness box all he could think about was how he hated the man who had humbled him in public. For the rest of the time he was thinking how he could take revenge, revenge in full and with interest. It must be done legally. He was not prepared to risk execution or imprisonment, though he would gladly have had the judge murdered had it been possible to do so without risk. But he knew that this could not be done. He knew, too, of the dangers of contempt of court. He had to get even with Mr Justice Beverley without risk to himself. It was not an easy problem, and it was not surprising that he did not do himself justice in giving evidence. He forgot all about Gilbert's case. He was no longer interested in it. He concentrated solely on finding a plan. The first paragraph in his appreciation was simple. Object: to wound Mr Justice Beverley as much and as often as possible. It was the remaining paragraphs which gave him so much trouble, and which made him give such fantastic evidence that Gilbert's chances of winning his action were tremendously increased. As soon as he left the witness box, he said to Mr Rounce: 'Settle this action on the best terms possible. I'm going.'

In consequence, after a few words between the solicitors, the action was settled on terms which were highly satisfactory to Gilbert, whose only remaining problem was whether he could persuade his local Inspector of Taxes not to treat the damages as income.

CHAPTER FIVE

The Law Reports

On the day after the trial Mr Bean sent for the Editor of the *London Clarion*.

'Frank,' he said, 'I've got a job for you.'

Frank waited. He had had many such jobs in his time. He was loyal to a degree and, as long as he received his salary from Clarion Newspapers Ltd, he did all he could to earn it. He sometimes disagreed with his chief, but never upon a matter of such importance that he was not able to disregard his own feelings and do exactly what was asked of him.

'I want you to find out all you can about Mr Justice Beverley.'

'You mean?'

'What I say. I want to know his history, whether there's anything against him and so forth. People don't advertise their faults in *Who's Who*. Not deliberately that is. I've already looked him up myself in most of the reference books but I don't think you'll find much to go on in them. Beverley has one son and one daughter, no clubs and no hobbies. His wife's alive and I gather he's only been married once. You might just check that though. Apparently he lives in the country. I don't suppose you'll find a thing, but put your best chaps on to it. Hunt around the village where he lives. High Court judges have occasionally been known to stray, though I doubt it in this case. I want it done at once. The next thing is more important. I don't want the first skimped, but I'm not expecting any dividends from it. I am from the second. I want you to send a reporter to sit permanently in his Court. Wherever he is, High Court, Old Bailey or on circuit, follow him round.'

'That's easy enough.'

'Of course. And the next part isn't difficult, but it'll want a good man to do it well and it'll require care. I want you to quote as often as possible in the *Clarion* something he says, particularly if he says something stupid. Even if it doesn't sound stupid in Court, it may look it in print. A sentence divorced from its context, for instance. Make him look a fool whenever you can. Put in a headline when you can. But be very careful to be absolutely accurate, and where you're leaving out anything in order to give the quotation more point, make sure it can't be contempt of court. I'll give you a list of counsel to consult. Send down to one of them in case of doubt and see that it's all right. Don't take any chances. But, subject to that, go for him. Don't give him a minute's peace. Make him frightened to open his mouth. Now, d'you follow what I want?'

'Absolutely. It should be quite amusing.'

'Yes. Get someone on to it who'll really enjoy picking up any bit of straw to make his bricks with. Start tomorrow and let's have the result of your search as soon as possible.'

Mr Bean was right in thinking that it was unlikely that even the most searching enquiries would show anything to the detriment of Mr Justice Beverley. He was a judge of the highest public and private reputation whose integrity had always been beyond question. He lived with his wife and daughter in the country, not far from London. He had a son who was an officer in the Regular Army. At the time of Mr Bean's instructions to the Editor, he had been on the Bench fourteen years and he was looking forward to his retirement in a year. He was very much looking forward to it. He had had a successful career at the Bar and was exceptionally happy in his marriage, but he had only been a judge some four years when his wife, whom he adored, was struck down with rheumatoid arthritis. She soon became a complete cripple requiring a day and night nurse to enable her to move. The judge spent all his savings on attempted cures. He investigated every new suggestion, trying qualified and unqualified men alike. Nothing apparently could be done. Having failed to find a cure he spent his whole time when he was not at work, and all his money, on making her life as comfortable as possible and he was always trying to devise new methods of giving her pleasure. She, in her turn, was devoted to her husband and was always trying to make him go out and do some of the things they enjoyed doing together but which it looked as though they would never be able to do again. She occasionally persuaded him to go to a theatre with a friend, but not often. The judge was looking forward to the time when he could retire so that he could spend nearly all his time with his wife. He had worked out his financial affairs so that he would just be able to do this on his pension. It would not be easy, as the expense of maintaining a household which would give his wife the maximum comfort was very great, but it could just be done, though only just. Mr Bean's reporters had no difficulty in finding out all this, and they found out nothing more, except that the judge's reputation for the strictest integrity could not have been higher.

'Well,' said Mr Bean, when he had been told that the search had been fruitless, 'that was only what I expected, but I'm quite pleased with young Howard's efforts.'

Howard was the reporter who had been put on to following the judge. On the first day on which he attended Mr Justice Beverley's Court, the judge was trying a case in which a customer of a restaurant had torn her dress on a protruding nail in a chair. In the course of the case the judge said: 'I know nothing about tintacks except that one end is sharp.'

This was translated by Howard into:

'JUDGE ON TINTACKS
"They are sharp."
Mr Justice Beverley.'

The cartoonist of the *London Clarion* used this on the following day by showing a thinly disguised Mr Justice Beverley in wig and gown taking the part of a yogi sitting on nails under the heading: 'Dammit, they *are* sharp.'

'Quite good for a beginning,' commented Mr Bean. 'Put it in "Best of the Week," ' he added, and so, in due course, there appeared in that paragraph:

' "One end of a tintack is sharp."
Mr Justice Beverley.'

A day or two later the judge tried an accident case where there had been a collision at cross roads. Both motorists had crossed in a well-recognised manner, that is, by slowing down slightly, hooting hard and then accelerating. They met in the middle, in the normal way. Each said the other had not hooted and each was full of righteous indignation at the deplorable driving of the other.

'When I try cases like this,' said Mr Justice Beverley, 'I sometimes think it would be a good thing if there were no hooters at all.'

This case was reported accurately under the heading:

'NO HOOTING FOR THE JUDGE'

A claim was brought by a landlord against a tenant for possession of a flat on the ground that the tenant had broken a covenant in his lease not to make an unreasonable noise. The landlord, who lived underneath, complained that the tenant was always using the piano, although he couldn't really play it. 'He goes on night after night, right up till midnight and after,' said the landlord. 'It would be bad enough if he played properly, but he doesn't. He just tickles the thing. It's more than I can stand.'

'This must stop,' was the eventual decision of Mr Justice Beverley, with the inevitable result that the *London Clarion* carried a report of the case under the heading:

' "STOP YOUR TICKLING"
Mr Justice Beverley.'

A little later on Howard had a piece of good fortune. No judge will try a case if he knows either of the parties. Even if he only had a nodding acquaintanceship with one of them. Even if the friendship or acquaintanceship ceased a long time ago. The reason is obvious. Should he decide in favour of the man or woman he knows, the person on the other side might think the trial had not been fair. Conversely, should he decide against the person he knew, that person might think that the judge had done so in order to show how fair-minded he was. Of course it is always possible that a judge may have known one of the parties to a case many years before and fail to recognise him or her by name or sight when the case is heard. Such accidental occurrences must happen occasionally, but judges do their best to prevent them from happening. Naturally some are more careful about this than others. Mr Justice Beverley was particularly scrupulous in this respect, and, if the name or face of a person seemed to strike some chord in his memory, he would mention the fact to counsel on each side before trying the case. One day he had a claim brought by an actress against another woman for breach of contract. The details of the claim do not matter. The actress was represented by counsel, the defendant was unrepresented and appeared for herself. Just as the case was being opened, the judge suddenly remembered that many years before he had known the actress. He had taken her out to dinner once, he had been to a tennis party at her house and had met her once or twice at other people's houses. It was at least twenty years before the trial.

'One moment, Mr Croft,' said the judge. 'Is not your client the actress of that name?'

Had both sides been represented by counsel, the judge would have simply beckoned to both of them to come up to the Associate's place below him. Then he would have explained the position to them, the case would have been sent to another judge, and there would have been nothing for the press to report. But with a litigant in person he did not feel he could take that course. The defendant would have wondered what on earth was happening if the judge beckoned her to come and speak to him on the Bench. He could have sent the Associate to explain the position to her and counsel opposing her, but, unluckily for him, he spoke before he thought of that course.

'Yes, my Lord,' replied counsel.

'I'm afraid I shan't be able to take this case then,' said the judge. 'I used to know the plaintiff.'

There was a whispered conversation between counsel and the actress.

'My client does not remember it,' said counsel, 'unless it was when she was at school.'

The judge was now regretting his hastiness in opening the subject publicly, but, having started, he had to go on.

'No, it was later than that. No, I'm afraid I shan't be able to take the case.'

Suddenly, in a loud whisper which everyone could hear, the actress was heard to say, 'Oh – it's the wig that does it.'

'Silence,' said the usher, but it was too late.

> 'IT WAS THE WIG THAT DID IT.
> JUDGE AND ACTRESS FRIEND.'

were the London Clarion's headlines above a completely accurate report of the facts.

This was a windfall for Howard. He had to work harder for the others. Nevertheless, he soon developed an ear for the remark which, though perfectly normal when said in Court, would tend to look ridiculous in print.

After a month or two of this kind of thing, the legal profession began to realise that this was a deliberate campaign against the judge. The Lord Chief Justice actually spoke to him on the subject, and suggested that although one isolated report would not amount to contempt of court, an obviously deliberate series of them would do so.

'If I don't mind,' said Mr Justice Beverley, 'I don't see why you should. They'll soon get tired of it, and it'll only play into their hands if proceedings are taken. The press and the Bench. The right to criticise a judge, and so forth. If they overstep the mark I suppose it might be necessary to do something about it, but, until then, I hope you'll leave it alone. Personally I find some of them quite amusing. Indeed, it gives my wife quite a lot of fun. She's always wondering what the latest will be. It's certainly good for me on the Bench. I speak better English and much less. As a matter of fact, I think a course of it for each new judge wouldn't be at all a bad idea.'

'All right,' said the Lord Chief Justice, 'I'll leave it for the moment, but I'm not going to have any judge made a laughing-stock.'

So the campaign of Mr Bean against Mr Justice Beverley went on until it suddenly led to something far more serious.

CHAPTER SIX

Sidney Has an Idea

Sidney York-Hanbury lay in bed calling for his breakfast. He was sometimes described as Sidney York, sometimes as Sidney Hanbury and sometimes by the two together. It all depended on what name he was using when he was arrested. A surname is the name by which a person is known, so that a man may change his name as often as he can get people to call him by another one. Sidney had not been born a York, a Hanbury or a York-Hanbury, but a plain Brown. Indeed, he still used that name from time to time, and in the files of Scotland Yard he had other names as well, but they were only temporary affairs.

'Hurry up, confound you,' he shouted.

'Coming.'

'You said that five minutes ago. For heaven's sake, get a move on.'

'Coming.'

'You'd better be.'

A minute or two later a woman came in with a piece of toast and some whisky in a glass.

'What the hell d'you call that?' he said, pointing to the glass.

'There isn't any more.'

'Then why the devil didn't you get some yesterday?'

'I hadn't any money.'

'Then why not ask me for some?'

'Last time you hit me when I did.'

'Did I hurt you?'

'Yes.'

'Well, it's nothing to what you'll get when I get up. How the hell d'you think I can manage on an eye-bath full? I bet you've been at it yourself.'

'I haven't – really.'

'Well – I'm going to treat you as if you had.' He drank what there was in the glass and glared angrily at her.

'I'll get some more as soon as it's time.'

'What with?'

'If you'll give me the money.'

'What's the time now?'

'Eleven o'clock.'

'Go and get some now. Give me the paper. Here's some money.' He threw two pound notes towards her.

'They won't let me take it away now.'

'Yes – they will – if no one else is in the shop. Wait till it's empty – then pop in. They know you.'

The woman went out and Sidney started to read the paper. It was the *London Clarion*. He glanced through it until he came to a report of one of Mr Justice Beverley's cases.

'Gosh, they've got it in for him,' he said aloud. Then, suddenly, a thought struck him. 'My godfathers,' he almost shouted. 'What a fool I've been.' Then. 'Martha, Martha,' he called. 'Oh – blast. You've gone out.'

Ten minutes later she was back and Sidney was able to finish his breakfast. The whisky, coupled with his new idea, made him almost affable. He put his arm round the woman and said: 'Look, old girl, I've got one hell of an idea.'

'Oh,' she said.

Her apathy did not worry Sidney. It was better like that. She was almost an animal, did what she was told, and accepted his blows or what, for lack of a more appropriate word, is called love, with hardly a murmur. He had owned her now for about six months and found her quite useful. For a man who was drinking himself to death he was curiously fond of women. Normally, at the stage he had reached, whisky or alcohol of some kind should have been the only thing he needed or wanted. But Sidney was the exception. And, of course, he also required looking after, feeding, putting to bed and so on, and a woman was useful for that too. So he had taken on Martha, and, from her point of view, it was no worse than any other job of the type she was likely to get.

'Look at this,' he said excitedly. 'Someone on that rag must hate his guts. Every day almost it's been going on. Why the hell didn't I think of it before?'

'What is it?'

'You'll see. I'm going to shave today. Got a call to pay. See I'm sober before I leave. Take the bottle away. No – let's just have a spot more. There. Now take it away. And if you let me have any more before I go out, I'll break the bottle over your head. I mean it. Now, come along, let's have some hot water. I'm going to shave.'

Two hours later Sidney called at the offices of the *London Clarion*.

'It's about Mr Justice Beverley,' he said. 'I want to see the Editor or someone.'

As soon as the Editor was told about Sidney, he sent for him.

'Good morning, and what can I do for you?'

'My name is York, Sidney York.'

'How d'you do? They said you'd called about Mr Justice Beverley.'

'That's right.'

'You're not his solicitor by any chance?'

'Oh – no – I've not come from him. Oh dear me, no. That's quite funny.'

'Well – Mr York – what is it?'

'I'm a commercial traveller, as a matter of fact.'

'I beg your pardon?'

'Yes – a commercial traveller. I sell things. I've got a line that I thought might interest you.'

'I see. A story, I presume. May I see it?'

'Not in writing yet. It's in here,' and he tapped his head. 'And before I uncork the bottle, I want to know what it's worth.'

'It depends what's in the bottle.'

'It's old, but good – very, very good.'

'Well, Mr York. Don't you think we might get down to brass tacks? I must know what it is you've got. You haven't told me a thing yet.'

'And I'm not going to either, till I've got an idea what it's worth.'

The Editor sighed. 'Very well,' he said. 'Excuse me a moment, would you?'

He left the room and sought Mr Bean. 'There's a pretty low type who says he's got something to sell about Beverley.'

'I'll see him. Show him in.'

'He's a little drunk, and it's very likely just a put-up job to get the price of some more.'

'Very likely, but I'll see him.' A few minutes later Sidney was shown into Mr Bean's room.

'This is a great honour,' he said. 'I'm not used to moving in these circles.'

'Sit down, Mr York,' said Mr Bean. 'You've something to sell, I gather.'

'That's right.'

'A story?'

'Right again.'

'About Mr Justice Beverley?'

'Another bull's eye.'

'Can you give me an idea what it is?'

'I could.'

'Now, look, Mr York, I never pay something for nothing. I'm quite prepared to pay generously for something I get, but I'll never pay anything in the hope of getting something.'

'Just suppose – only suppose, mind you, I could tell you a story about Mr Justice Beverley that would make his hair stand on end – what would you pay for it?'

'Nothing at all if you couldn't prove it was true.'

'Supposing I could?'

'Well – I've told you. I'm not mean. We pay well for anything in the nature of news. And, at the moment, Mr Justice Beverley is news.'

'So I gather. How much?'

'Well – of course – it must depend on the story, but something in the region of £500 perhaps.'

'£500? That isn't much.'

'I don't know what you've got to sell, if anything.'

'Assume it's something you'd give your eyes for.'

'Well, if it were really something good, I dare say we'd pay £1,000 or so – perhaps even more.'

Sidney got up. 'Thank you very much,' he said. 'That's just what I wanted to know.'

'What *is* this?' asked Mr Bean. 'Aren't you interested?'

'Most interested. But there are other papers, you know – and other people.'

'I'm not going to take part in an auction,' said Mr Bean. 'Aren't you?' said Sidney. 'As a matter of fact, that's exactly what you are going to do. Good morning.' And, leaving the office, he went straight to a railway station where he bought a ticket for Pemberton. This was the nearest station to Murrell Keeping, the small village where, according to *Who's Who*, Mr Justice Beverley lived.

CHAPTER SEVEN

Sidney's Idea Continued

Lady Beverley's new day nurse had been on the telephone for some minutes before the front door bell rang for the second time. She did not hear it when it was first rung. On the other hand, Sidney could hear through the open window everything that she said. And this is what he had heard: 'Hullo. Could I have 35, please. Oh, yes, thank you. As comfortable as can be expected. Yes, they do say the new drug works wonders. Yes, I have read about it. No, I don't know if they're going to try it. I've only just come here, you know. No, 35, please – the chemist, Mr Bolton. Thank you so much. Yes, I'll tell Sir John you enquired. Yes, he is. Yes – they all are. Of course, I've only known them such a short time, but I do agree. Yes, Sister Brighton was here a long time. No – I didn't really know her. Just met her, you know. My name? Paignton. Sally Paignton. Yes, would you mind? I think it's 35, but I'll have to look it up again. Yes, of course, you would know. I didn't think there'd be two chemists. Yes, it is a small place. No, I wasn't born in London, but I've lived there a long time. No, as a matter of fact, I do come from the West Country. Yes, it is a coincidence about my name. No, I wasn't born there. I wonder if you'd mind – Exeter, as a matter of fact. Yes, Exmoor is lovely. Thank you *so* much. Yes, it is a little important. Some sleeping tablets. Yes, Dr Sanderstead seems very nice. Your back? Oh, dear, I'm so sorry. A slipped disc? He says there isn't such a thing. Well, some doctors believe in them and some don't. Yes, it just depends on the doctor. Yes, backache does sound nicer – but I wonder if you'd be so terribly kind as to – oh, that is good of you. Oh, no, not at all. I've enjoyed our chat. Yes, I do enjoy one. Yes, it does make the day go quicker. Look here – don't worry about the call. I'll just slip round – oh, but there's no one else in the house at the moment. Oh, thank you. No, not really urgent. Just quite, you know. I want to be certain to have them before tonight. Yes, very well, thank you so much. Hullo – hullo – oh, good afternoon. I wonder if you'd be kind enough to send round some more sleeping tablets for Lady Beverley. Your reference number is – oh – the butcher – I'm so sorry – I must have given the wrong number. Exchange – Exchange – oh – there's the bell again. Excuse me. I'll be back.'

She put down the receiver and went to the front door.

'I'm so sorry. Have you been waiting long? No one else is in, and I was on the 'phone.'

'That's quite all right, quite all right,' said Sidney. 'No hurry at all.'

'Who is it you wanted to see? Sir John isn't back from Court yet.'

'No, of course, he wouldn't be. I did want to see him, as a matter of fact. When does he usually get back?'

'About six, I think. But I've only been here a couple of days.'

'Is there any other member of the family I could see for the moment?'

'I'm afraid not. Lady Beverley, of course, is in bed, and Miss Beverley's out. I don't know when she'll be back. Oh

– they are expecting Sir John's son home some time today, but I've no idea when. I'm so sorry to be so useless.'

'Not at all, not at all. You're most kind,' said Sidney, who was charmed with her appearance. 'By the way, d'you happen to know what the licensing hours are in these parts? The Bull seemed very much closed when I passed it.'

'I'm terribly sorry. I'm afraid I don't even know that. Perhaps you'd call back again later? I'm afraid I must go back and telephone. Will you excuse me? Can I give any name?'

'Yes – thank you. York's the name. Sidney York. Well – I'll take a stroll and come back later.'

By this Sidney meant that he would go and sit in the porch of the Bull until the bars opened. He left the judge's house while Sally went back and at last made her telephone call successfully. She had just finished when a man whom she rightly took to be the gardener put his head round the French windows of the room where she had telephoned.

'Hullo,' he said, in an educated voice. 'You're new.'

'Hullo,' said Sally, 'I'm the new day nurse. Who are you, may I ask?'

'You certainly may. As a matter of fact, I'm two people really. At the moment I'm the gardener. Two days a week. Two hours a day. Two bob an hour. Trim your hedge, dig your potatoes and all that. Tonight I shall put on a suit, and come to dinner – that's if I'm asked.'

'I see. It sounds a pleasant existence.'

'It is a pleasant existence. Much better than secretary of a golf club. More independent. And I don't mind telling you I trim a very pretty hedge and dig a very pretty potato. Brain's the name, Willie Brain.'

'I'm Sally Paignton.'

'You're an improvement on the last, if I may say so.'

'I don't think you may. It's not very polite to either of us.'

'I'm sorry, Sally. I apologise. I may call you Sally, mayn't I? I'm old enough to be your father, grandfather even. And, anyway, no one takes any notice of me. A good chap Willie Brain, they say, but just a bit – and then they tap their heads – but quite harmless, they're good enough to add – oh – yes, quite harmless. And all because I do a spot of gardening to help the old pension out.'

'I think you're very sensible.'

'Thank you, Sally. That's what I like to hear. Haven't heard anyone say that for years. Let me see – thirty years, it must be – it was my Colonel – that's right – "You're a sensible chap, Brain," I remember him saying – and he was an old fool if ever there was one. Black-eyed Susan, we used to call him. I could never make out why. No one could – but Black-eyed Susan he remained. Funny how people get called names and no one knows the reason.'

'Well – I shall be called something if I don't get back to my patient.'

Sally went back to Lady Beverley and Colonel Brain made himself at home in an armchair. He had been in the neighbourhood for about a year and, once people had got used to the idea of employing a retired Colonel, he obtained all the work he wanted as a part-time gardener. He was quite good at it, although he never overworked. He explained this from the start to his customers.

'Two bob an hour's below the rate,' he told them, 'but it includes what I call "breathers". How many breathers an hour? All depends on the weather and how comfortable the chairs are. But you'll find it works out all right by and large. Willie Brain won't let you down – not so that you'd notice.' His breather on this occasion lasted ten minutes. He was just getting up to go back when the judge's son James arrived.

'Thank heaven,' said the Colonel. 'How are you, Jimmy?'

'Fine, thanks. And you?'

'Mustn't grumble, you know. A bit of the old backache. Just having a breather. What's the news with you? Tell me something to stop me going back to work. Anything will do.'

'I hear they've got a new nurse. What's she like or haven't you seen her yet?'

'I was going to say pretty as a picture. But lots of pictures aren't at all pretty. Hang 'em sideways or upside down and you wouldn't know the difference. I like to know what I'm looking at. I asked an artist fellow once what it was all in aid of. Quite a nice chap. You may have known him. Lived round here when I first came. "What's it meant to be?" I said. "Ah," he said, and looked knowing, or as though he wasn't sure if he could hear the telephone. Nothing more happened for a time. So I looked at it again. "Is it meant to be anything particular?" I went on. "Your guess is as good as mine," he said. "Have a try." He was quite a good chap and I wanted the job of mowing his lawn. I couldn't even begin to guess without hurting his feelings – I'd have said, "Is it Grape-Nuts outside a bathing machine?" That wouldn't have done. So I tried another way. "I'll tell you what," I said. "There's something about the paint. The way you use it, I mean." "Ah," he said, obviously pleased. It was plainly the right line to go on. "It looks like velvet," I said. "It's meant to look like paint," he said. He left the neighbourhood soon after that, so I didn't lose much – I got the job from his successor. He'd got his feet on the ground all right. No nonsense about him.'

'Who d'you mean?'

'Old Archie Preston, the Coroner. He doesn't get much work in these parts. Too many natural deaths. We could do with the odd murder or two. Liven the place up a bit.'

'What's this nurse like, apart from her looks? Nice girl, d'you think?'

'Seems charming. No airs. Natural. That's how I like 'em. Natural. After all, I say, that's what we are, aren't we, so why not be it, if you follow me?' After a little further conversation, Colonel Brain mentioned that his housekeeper was away for a couple of nights.

'How are you managing about meals?'

'Oh, I manage, you know; the old sardine and all that.'

'Why don't you dine with us tonight, Colonel? I'm sure father'd be pleased.'

'Well, that's really most kind of you, my dear fellow. I should love to come. Fact is, when she went, my housekeeper said: "Go and put your head on one side at the Beverleys. That'll do you for one meal." She was right, as usual, thanks to you my dear fellow.'

'What was the rest of her advice?'

'Well, as a matter of fact, she did suggest I should help the vicar's wife with the flowers, and give some tomatoes to the doctor.'

'So you won't need the old sardine after all.'

'In reserve, my dear fellow, in reserve. Never commit your reserves until you're quite sure they're needed. That's how I failed the Staff College as a matter of fact. I remember one of the examining Generals asking me: "But how can you control the battle if you've committed your reserves?"

' "By using my initiative, sir," I said. I thought that was rather good. After all, it's what we'd been taught from the time I joined the Army. Initiative – use your initiative – always take the initiative. Yes, I must say I thought I'd done rather well. It was a bit awkward about the reserves. I thought I'd one more brigade than I had. After all, it's the sort of thing that does happen in battle. It's one thing to do it in the drawing room, and quite another on the battlefield, with metal flying in all directions. So I thought I'd slipped out of that one rather well, except that I didn't quite like the tone of his voice when he said: "Doing what?"

' "Using my initiative, sir," I repeated. He seemed puzzled for the moment. Then he said: "In what direction?"

'I'd got the answer for that – at least I thought it was good enough. "In all directions," I said. He didn't ask me any more questions after that. "I see," he said and then he put his monocle in his eye, and walked away. He whispered to the officer who was with him, as they left. I could have sworn I heard him say – not that I was listening, my dear fellow, but these things carry – I could have sworn I heard him say: "Pass that man," but apparently it wasn't. I knew it was a mistake, committing those reserves, as soon as I'd done it, but I thought I'd got away with it. Still, there it is, my dear fellow. Now you see why I'm careful with the sardines.'

'Absolutely,' said James. 'I hope the doctor was pleased with the tomatoes.'

'Oh – very, my dear fellow. More than your father would be if he could see me gossiping with you. Two bob an hour this is costing him – apart from the dinner – that's the trouble with the working man today – you've got to watch him all the time.'

So Colonel Brain went back to his work and James went in to see his mother.

'Do take your father up to town once anyway, Jimmy,' she said. 'It's not good for him being here all the time.'

'I'll try, mother, but you know what he is. I'm told the new nurse is pretty.'

'Yes – she is. But I said take your *father* up to town. Or, if *he'd* take her out, that really would be something. It would do him a world of good.'

'Me, too.'

'You don't need it, Jimmy, and he does.'

They continued chatting for some little time. Then the bell rang. Apparently there was no one available to answer it as it rang again, and then again.

So James went to the door. It was Sidney, a little refreshed but looking for more.

'Good evening,' he said. 'Can you tell me when Sir John Beverley will be home?'

'In about an hour, I should think. Can I do anything for you? I'm his son.'

'That's most kind. May I come in for a moment? I'm an old friend of your father, but we haven't met for years.'

'Please do.'

James took Sidney into the drawing room. 'Please sit down.'

'Thank you.'

As soon as he had sat down Sidney looked round the room to see if there was any sign of a drink. It soon became fairly obvious that he was doing so. James knew there was none. It was one of his father's economies not to have any drink in the house except a few bottles of wine for use on special occasions. This was certainly not a special occasion. There was an embarrassing silence. Eventually they both started to speak at once.

'I suppose – ' began Sidney.

'I'm afraid – ' began James.

'I'm sorry,' went on James, 'you were going to say?'

'You haven't such a thing as a whisky, I suppose? Got a dreadful thirst. Gassed, you know. It takes me like this.'

'I'm most awfully sorry, but we haven't a drop in the house.'

'Good gracious!'

'I'm so sorry,' said James. There was an uncomfortable silence. It was broken by Sidney saying: 'Well, what about a drop of gin, then?'

'I'm terribly sorry. We haven't any.'

'He usedn't to be a teetotaller.'

'He isn't. But I'm afraid there just isn't any. Actually the only thing I can offer you is – '

'Well,' said Sidney, 'half a loaf – you know – any port in a storm – that's it, of course, port. You couldn't have a judge's house without port. Mellows the speech, if not the sentence. Thank you very much, my dear chap. Haven't had vintage port for a long time. Most kind of you. What is it, by the way?'

'How long is it since you saw my father?'

'Thirty-five years or more. But what's that got to do with it? Let's get down to brass tacks. I'm a thirsty man. I want a drink.'

'I'm afraid I can only offer you water or lemon squash.'

Sidney grimaced.

'My dear chap, if that's a joke, I think it's in pretty poor taste. I'm sure your father wouldn't approve. He's a generous fellow, if ever there was one. Unless he's changed.'

'My dear Mr – Mr – ' began James.

'York – Sidney York. Your father and I fought together in the First World War. I'm sure he wouldn't want you to turn me empty away.'

James had had enough by this time and could not resist saying: 'Empty?'

'Empty – as far as you're concerned. I must say I think it's a bit thick. I suppose I'd better get back to the Bull until your father comes.'

'I think perhaps you should. But I'm not at all sure that my father will be able to see you.'

'Oh – he'll see me all right. He wouldn't forget an old battle comrade.'

'That remains to be seen, Mr York. I'm beginning to wonder if you ever knew my father at all.'

'Are you really now? Just because he's a judge – and I'm a – I'm a – well – I haven't done so well as he has – though I have made a bit free of tax in my time – that doesn't alter the fact that we fought side by side – side by side – I assure you. Pretty bloody awful it was too. But you wouldn't know. Your war was a cake-walk compared with ours.'

'So I've been told.'

'By your father?'

'No.'

'He did pretty well, as a matter of fact. Picked up a DSO as a captain. Not bad. No, I've a great admiration for your father. He's deserved his success.'

'Thank you.'

Eventually James managed to get rid of Sidney. He had only just done so when his sister Judy came in.

'Jimmy,' she said, 'who was that curious creature who stumbled out of the gate just before I came in?'

'No idea. Says he was in the Army; with father, but I doubt it. On a cadging expedition, I suspect. What's the news with you?'

'Lots and lots of news. I'm engaged. Isn't it lovely?'

'Bernard Kent?'

'Yes. D'you know, I nearly had one of my fainting fits when he asked me, but I just managed to hold on.'

'That was a bit of luck. He might have changed his mind by the time you came round. But – seriously – did you? Are you all right?'

'Absolutely. It was just one of those things. It's time I had another, as a matter of fact. It's several years since the last. They don't mean a thing. The specialist said so. Now I must go and tell mother.'

While Judy was discussing with her mother her engagement to Bernard Kent, who was an Assistant Commissioner at Scotland Yard – which discussion necessarily included such matters as the choice of trousseau, church, names for children (up to three) godparents and kindred matters – Sidney was slowly but steadily drinking himself into a state of affability and self-confidence. It was not that he lacked self-confidence in the ordinary way but he appreciated that rather a lot was required of a man who intended to extract an annual income, or at least a large capital sum, out of a Queen's Bench judge by threats. He was quite looking forward to the experience, which was not only new to him but which, he thought, was probably being done for the first time. Nevertheless, he appreciated that it would doubtless require a certain amount of tact and that judges are not people whom it is easy to frighten by threats. But then, of course, he told himself, normally the threat is an idle one. His would be far from idle. It was plain that, if the judge would not buy, Alexander Bean would. It was a pleasant thought. He had seldom been so pleased with himself. He had never been on such a certain winner. It was only a question of amount. It was even better than his last long firm fraud, though he had got away with that quite comfortably. It would be, it was true, about as mean an act as even Sidney could have devised. But when a man reaches Sidney's stage he cannot afford to moralise. There were three questions he considered before embarking on an adventure – the first, is it feasible? the second, will it be profitable? the third, am I likely to get caught? All other considerations were irrelevant. This did not mean that he was not aware of the extent of his viciousness. On the contrary, he obtained some pleasure from an appreciation of it. 'I rather think,' he said to himself, 'for pure unadulterated beastliness this will take a lot of beating. Sidney, you're a real bad hat – I venture to say that you have no redeeming feature more power to your elbow.'

'Another double Scotch, please, miss,' he said aloud.

Meanwhile, wholly unaware that Sidney was about to call on him or what it would mean, Mr Justice Beverley was on his way home. He had just bought some new records for his wife and he was looking forward to seeing her pleasure on hearing them.

'Yes,' he said to one of his regular travelling companions, 'I shall finish in a year. Oh – yes – I've enjoyed the life – but it'll give me more time to be with my wife.'

'Won't you find your life rather empty with no cases to try – or will you retry some of those you've tried in the past?'

'Oh, dear me, no. I might come to a different conclusion and that might be worrying. Although, of course, it wouldn't be any use worrying at that stage. I can't say, though, that I ever have worried about my cases after they're over. That sort of thing is no good to a judge. Do your best and, when it's over, forget it. If you've made a mistake, that's just too bad. That's what the Court of Appeal is for. To put me right. Ah – here we are. Good night.'

About half an hour later Sidney went back to the judge's house. Judy's engagement and the new nurse had put Sidney out of James' mind until the bell rang.

'Oh, that'll be that fellow again,' he said. 'I forgot to tell you. Some bounder who says he was in the Army with you, father. What was his name? I know – York – Sidney York. On a cadging expedition, I suspect.'

'York?' repeated the judge. 'It doesn't ring a bell. You see him first, Jimmy. Ask him which battalion we were in together. If he gets it wrong, say I'm too busy and tell him to write. If he gets it right, I'll see him. I'd never like to send away a chap who really had been with me.'

A few minutes later Sidney was brought to the judge. He saw him alone in the dining room. Swaying slightly, but otherwise with cheerful confidence, Sidney went towards the judge, with outstretched hand. It was obvious that he was not recognised.

'Johnny boy, you've forgotten me. You've gone and forgotten me.'

'I'm afraid – ' began the judge.

'I suppose I have changed a bit. But not as much as all that surely. You haven't. P'raps it's the name. That has varied since we last met.'

'I haven't the faintest idea who you are. I'm sorry.' Having regard to Sidney's condition, the judge did not speak genially.

'I've read all about you lots of times. You may have read a bit about me too. But then, of course, the name's been different. Never been in front of you, though. That'd have been awkward.'

'I'm sorry,' said the judge, 'would you mind telling me who you are and what you want? I haven't a lot of time to spare.'

'Johnny boy, what a reception. Not that I'm really surprised. We did go rather different ways after 1918. Does Brown mean anything to you?'

'Brown?' repeated the judge, rather irritably. He wanted to get back to his wife. Then, suddenly, he did remember a Brown – a Sidney Brown, too. He looked at Sidney – and at last saw the faintest signs of the man he had once known.

'You're getting it, Johnny boy. C Company. Remember? Does the name Hélène help to bring it back to you?'

'Yes – I do remember now. I did read about you once, too.'

Sidney's first conviction had been in the name of Brown, and, from the description, the judge had recognised his fellow officer. He had expected an appeal for help when he came out of prison. He was rather surprised when it did not come. Still, he had been an independent chap. However, here he was now. But he'd certainly taken a long time about it. He couldn't have been in prison all the time.

'If you'd wanted to see me, why haven't you been before? Why have you waited till now?'

'Nothing to see you for, old boy. You'd have just thought I was on a cadging expedition.' He paused for a moment. 'That's what you think now, isn't it? Come on, Johnny boy. Be honest, that's what you think, isn't it?'

'It had occurred to me.'

'Well – you're wrong, Johnny boy. Dead wrong. I've never cadged yet. A good many other things – but not that. I won't be beholden to anyone.'

'Then what is it you want?'

'Why so fast, old boy? Aren't you pleased to see me? Don't you want to discuss old times? There's lots we could talk about. You're a judge, I know. And I'm a well –

whatever you like to call me – but we did serve together – didn't we, Johnny boy – and I did do you a bit of good once or twice, didn't I now?'

'That's perfectly true.'

'Well – then why come the old acid? Not even a "Sit down, old man – what's it going to be?" That isn't like you, Johnny boy. I'm disappointed.'

'I'm sorry – but thirty-five years is a long time. We have gone different ways, and I'm afraid now we haven't much in common. I confess that, if you hadn't been half drunk, I should have been more affable. But, as it is, you can't expect much of a welcome in your condition. And, as you haven't come cadging – for which you certainly have my respect – hadn't you better go?'

Sidney's answer was to flop down in a chair. 'Sorry, old boy, I'm tired,' he said. Then, quite casually, he added: 'The *Clarion* seems to have its knife into you.' The judge did not reply.

'I went to see the Editor, as a matter of fact. Said I thought it was a shame. I saw Bean himself, d'you know that? The great Alexander Bean. What d'you think of it? He actually saw me himself.'

'Why are you telling me all this? I'm not in the least interested in Alexander Bean or the *Clarion*.'

'No? But they're very interested in you.'

'What of it?'

'They wanted me to sell them a story.' Sidney paused. 'A story about you. D'you know what they offered? £5,000. I said: "That's ridiculous. The old boy would pay more than that himself." I meant you. Not very respectful, I know – but out of Court we talk of judges like that. As a matter of fact, we're not always as polite as that.'

The judge got up. 'Get out at once,' he said.

'Now, Johnny, don't be silly,' said Sidney. 'There's no point in taking offence.'

'Get out.'

'Look, Johnny. I'd really much prefer to sell it to you. It'd look horrid in the *Clarion*. And they'd really take it, you know. Do give yourself a chance.'

'If you don't get out, I shall have you put out.'

'Oh, dear, you're so impetuous. Well – I suppose – if you insist – I shall have to go.' He got up slowly. 'But you see,' he added, 'I wasn't on a cadging expedition. Squeezing's more the word, isn't it? Why don't you hit me, Johnny? You'd get off, I'm sure, if the beaks knew why. Go on – have a go – try that candlestick. I deserve it, don't I? The lowest of the low. Blackmailing a judge. That's pretty bad, Johnny. Would I get more for that? Shall I ring the police? I'll make a statement, you know – a full statement. Imprisonment for life – isn't it? Well – why don't you do something about it? You don't even push me out. Shall I call on the village policeman on the way back to the station and send him to you?'

'If you don't leave the house at once, I shall have you put out.'

'But – Johnny – if there's a disturbance and it gets into court – it'll be so bad for you. You'd have to resign, wouldn't you? I'd hate that to happen. Wouldn't do me any good. Wouldn't do you any good either. On the other hand – if you just make a reasonable offer – oh – Johnny – don't leave me.'

But the judge left the room and spoke to James.

'Jimmy – you'll have to get rid of that chap, I'm afraid.'

'I'm not surprised. I thought that was it.'

'It's rather worse. I'll have to tell you about it later. But I don't want a scene. Try and get him out quietly. Don't have a fight. We'll have to ring Parsons, if necessary. But don't, if you can help it. And I don't want a noise – or it may worry your mother.'

'OK, father. I'll deal with it.'

But dealing with Sidney was not so easy. He was sitting comfortably in an armchair.

'Mr York, I understand my father's ordered you out of this house. Would you mind going?'

'I would rather. I'm comfortable. Nice chairs here.'

'I don't want to have to call the village policeman, you know.'

'My dear boy – I offered to ring him for your father – and he didn't seem to want me to.'

'What is it you want?'

'Ah – that's much more sociable. Well – apart from a drink – which I gather there's not much chance of getting in this house – apart from a drink – I want money.'

'Well, you're not going to get any.'

'Now – how on earth d'you know that? I may not get any here – but, if I don't get it here, I'll get it somewhere else.'

'All right – go and get it, but leave here, please.'

'You don't know what you're saying, my boy. It wouldn't do your father any good at all if I did that. You see – I don't want money for nothing – oh dear, no – I've something to sell – the *Clarion*'s made me an offer and I thought your father might go one better.'

'He certainly won't. I don't know what you're talking about, but if you think my father or any of us mind what the *Clarion* reports about him, you're very much mistaken. If you've a funny story about him, you go and sell it, but get out of here.'

'Well – you're quite right, I have a story – a very funny story – but it's a true story too. And when I've gone – just you ask your father if he'd like it published in the *Clarion*.

If he won't buy it – perhaps you would. Or perhaps you've a rich uncle who'd like it. I'll give you my address in case you want to get hold of me – you remember the name – don't you – York – Sidney York – and the address 12 Touchstone Street, WC. Just you drop me a line or come and see me – in the next forty-eight hours, if you feel like it. No use coming after that – as the goods will have been sold. It's a pity the *Clarion* hates your father so. I don't, you know. No reason to at all. On the contrary, he did me a very good turn once. A very good turn indeed. Ask him to tell you about it before you read about it in the *Clarion*. It'd come better from him. Now, I really will be off. No, don't bother to see me out. I can manage. And I won't pinch the spoons. I want something better than that.'

CHAPTER EIGHT

Colonel Brain's Complaint

As Sidney York went unsteadily towards the Bull he talked to himself.

'I'm not sure, old boy,' he said, 'that you've been very sensible about this. Suppose you have to sell to the *Clarion*, the old man may run you in for blackmail and there'll be two witnesses against you. You'll get a lifer, you know. I can hear the judge smacking his lips as he says it. "Despicable beyond belief – public must be protected – only one sentence for a man like you." Very reasonable, very reasonable indeed. "Have I anything to say why sentence should not be passed on me according to law?" Not a thing. Deserve it all, old boy. Just carry on. Don't take any notice of me. Now pull yourself together. If I sell to the *Clarion*, I must disappear. South America. Mr Bean will have to arrange it. He will. But if Johnny boy – or that fine upstanding son of his – will make an offer, I think that would be better – yes – on the whole I think that would be better. But I can't very well approach them again. Or can I? I'll sleep on it. Pity I've got to go back to town. Still, I can sleep in the train. At the moment I must say sleep seems to me a very good thing, a very good thing indeed.'

While Sidney was considering the next step to be taken, Mr Justice Beverley was taking his son and daughter into his confidence. He told them the whole story. In the First World War he and Sidney had fought together in France, and from time to time they had helped each other. It was true, too, that on one occasion when the judge – then a young man of twenty-one – had gone out with a patrol and was overdue back, Sidney had taken a couple of men to try and find him. He did find him in a very sticky position, and by a combination of courage and good sense Sidney got him out of it. Naturally the young Beverley was extremely grateful. Not long afterwards he had an opportunity of showing the extent of his gratitude. The battalion had been taken out of the line to have a short rest. In the course of his rest Sidney had misbehaved himself with a young woman called Hélène, who was the daughter of the local mayor. It was not a particularly disgraceful affair, but Hélène's parents discovered it, reported the matter to the military authorities and, in the result, Sidney was charged with conduct unbecoming an officer and a gentleman. The main piece of evidence against him was that of the parents, who said they had come upon him with their daughter at night and that he had run away. They had only seen him once before, but they felt sure of his identity. Hélène, who was of a kindly nature and had a sense of humour of which her parents strongly disapproved, supported Sidney's defence, denied that she had ever had anything to do with him, though perhaps she might have smiled at him once in the street, in mistake for another officer to whom she had been introduced. She admitted that she had been with a young man of Sidney's build, but it was not Sidney. Indeed, she did not know who it was. 'I know,' she said, 'that it was very naughty of me, as I had never been introduced to him.' But the mayor and mayoress were positive in their identification and it was fairly obvious that the amiable Hélène was protecting someone – probably Sidney. His defence was an alibi and he asked the young Beverley to support him in it.

'If you could say we were together in the billet all the evening, with the necessary corroborative detail, I'd get away with it easily.'

Perjury is, of course, a very serious offence, but, to a young man just out of the firing-line and about to go back there again very shortly, it did not appear such a terrible thing to tell a lie in order to assist another young man in the same position as himself. Probably they would both be killed anyway. In any event, Hélène, though only nineteen, had been a willing party to the evening's entertainment, and, had she not been the daughter of the mayor, probably nothing would have happened. So the young Beverley agreed to help. It is true that he did feel extremely uncomfortable just after he had taken the oath. There was a solemnity about the matter which he had not appreciated when he had agreed to give evidence. But, having gone so far, he did not feel he could go back on his word to Sidney. So he gave the necessary evidence and Sidney was acquitted. Of course it was a very wrong thing to do, but there were strong mitigating circumstances. His age, the uncertainty of life at the time and the fact that he had nothing to gain from the crime himself. He had felt a little uncomfortable about it for a time, but it was not very long before he was able to dismiss it as one of the peccadilloes which most people commit during a lifetime. And now, nearly forty years afterwards, Sidney, of all people, having noticed the London *Clarion*'s campaign against the judge, proposed to blackmail him because of it.

'But I can't think what you're worried about, father,' said James. 'Surely the *Clarion* wouldn't dare publish the story.'

'I don't suppose even the *Clarion* would without writing to me first …'

'Writing to you? What for?'

'To ask me whether the story was true.'

'Well, that's simple enough,' said James. 'You tell them it isn't. They wouldn't dare publish after that,' said James.

'Surely James is right, Daddy,' put in Judy. 'There's only his word that you gave the evidence about the alibi. And who'd believe him against you? And then he couldn't swear it was untrue without admitting that he'd himself committed perjury, could he?'

'Well, that's true, but it wouldn't hurt him to admit perjury as a matter of fact. He couldn't be charged with any offence so long after he left the Army.'

'Nor could you then, Daddy.'

'That's perfectly true, but it isn't really the point. There are two things neither of you seem to appreciate. First – that, if the *Clarion* asked me if the allegation were true, I couldn't deny it.'

'Why on earth not?'

'Because it's true.'

'But it's perfectly outrageous. You do the chap a good turn and then, forty years afterwards, he tries to blackmail you because of it.'

'You don't have to enlarge on that aspect of it, I assure you. It's quite unspeakable – but I'm not twenty-one any more – I'm not just out of the firing-line – I can't lie about it if I'm asked – even though I lied on oath at the court martial.'

'Well – I'll answer the letter and lie for you, father. It wouldn't be on my conscience.'

'I dare say it wouldn't, Jimmy, but that sort of thing just can't be done. That leads me to the second point you seem to be missing. The seriousness of the allegation. I don't suppose it would matter very much to most people. But you can't have a High Court judge on the Bench who's committed perjury – even forty years ago.'

'But you are on the Bench, Daddy – and you say you did.'

'Well – that's true,' said the judge, 'you have a point there. I should amend what I said to who's known to have committed perjury however long ago. Just think what the *Clarion* could do with it. I'd have to resign. There's no doubt about it.'

'Well – you're not going to,' said James. 'I'll eat my hat if Judy and I'll let you.'

'I certainly don't want to if I can avoid it – not till I've earned my pension – but I couldn't avoid it if it came out. How could I sit on the Bench and say, "I don't believe a word the witness says" or warn a witness of the dangers of committing perjury when everyone knew that I'd done it myself. No, Master York was right when he said the *Clarion* would like it. It'd be an absolute godsend for them. If they published it without asking me if it were true, I couldn't take proceedings against them because I couldn't dispute it. If I didn't take proceedings, I'd have to resign. If they do write and ask me before publishing, it comes to the same thing as I can't dispute it. No, I'm afraid it's a dreadful situation. Don't for heaven's sake tell your mother. I'll have to think it over. At the moment I haven't the faintest idea what to do.'

The judge went back to his wife, and James and Judy started to discuss the matter.

'We've got to do something about this, Judy. I didn't realise how desperate it was at first.'

'I agree, but what can we do? You'll never persuade father to lie about it. And I suppose he's right in saying that, once it's made public, he'd have to resign. How the devil he'd be able to look after himself and mother without a pension, heaven alone knows.'

'We've just got to stop it being published,' said James.

'What d'you suggest?' said Judy.

'I can't think of anything. As far as I can see, we're absolutely in this chap's hands as long as he's alive.'

'That's an idea. Why not run him over while he's lurching all over the street?'

'I would for two pins, I really would. But it's too dangerous. I might be found out and that'd be worse for them.'

'Anyway – I suppose it is rather ridiculous to think of murder.'

'I don't know why. It's equally ridiculous to think of father being blackmailed – and by the man he got off – and because he got him off. Really it makes my blood boil. The fellow ought to be killed. I've killed far better chaps than him in the war.'

'I quite agree, but we want to be practical. I've just got engaged and I'm going to be married. I don't want to go and get hanged first.'

'You know, the more I think of it, the more I like the idea. If I could do it without being found out, I would. Dammit, when I came home from the war the village turned out to greet me, led by the vicar. Just because I'd killed quite a lot of Germans. Now, if they found out I'd killed this chap, who's infinitely worse than any German I killed, they'd have me arrested. It doesn't make sense. This chap ought to be destroyed. And just because there isn't a war on and he isn't an enemy, I can't do it. He's a pest to society. He'll obviously die of drink anyway fairly soon.

He's no good to himself or anyone else. I'd bump him off if I got the chance and it wouldn't be on my conscience. It'd be less of a crime than dangerous driving. Then you might kill someone decent. If only the police weren't so particular about murder. They take an awful lot of trouble to find out who did it. Can you think of any way we could do it without being caught? After all, it was your suggestion in the first place.'

'I wasn't serious.'

'Well – be serious. Tell me really – would it be on your conscience if we got rid of him?'

'I don't know about conscience – but I have an instinctive feeling against it. A mixture of the Ten Commandments and the danger of getting caught, I suppose.'

'I wish I knew what that particular Commandment meant. I went out killing Germans just because a number of men – not God – but a number of men in Downing Street said: "Off you go boy, kill Germans, and good luck to you. The only good German is a dead German." I'm not complaining. I think they were right. But there's nothing in the Ten Commandments about exceptions if the Government of the day says "kill". I agree that in peacetime you can't have people killing people unofficially – it has to be made a crime. But the only crime in this case would be being found out. D'you think we could get him to the edge of a cliff and push him over? That's a very good method if you run for help immediately.'

'I can't see him coming to the edge of a cliff with you.'

'Shooting's no good, poison's hopeless. I can't stick a knife into him or bang him on the head. I think your idea of running him down is the best, but it's pretty tricky and you could never tell if there were some awkward witnesses. I really don't know, Judy. What the devil are we to do?'

At that moment they were interrupted by Colonel Brain, who burst into the room in a dishevelled state, talking loudly and almost incoherently. Eventually they calmed him and persuaded him to sit down.

'Where's your father?' said the Colonel. 'Must talk to him. Evidence and all that. Just been assaulted.'

'Assaulted, Colonel? What's it all about and who did it?'

"Pon my word, I've never heard of such a thing. I could have sworn it couldn't happen.'

'But what has happened?'

'If your father had told me it had happened, I would have said to him – looking him full in the face – I would have said: "It could not happen in Murrell Keeping." Mind you, your father's a fine man. I shouldn't doubt his word, but that's what I should have said: "It could not happen in Murrell Keeping." Don't you agree?'

'But we don't know what it is, Colonel.'

'But I've just told you, my dear girl,' went on the Colonel. 'Assault, battery and all that.'

'Who assaulted you?'

'Terrible fellow he was. Seven foot tall, I should say – not less – bright ginger hair and a face – well, my dear fellow, we had some odd ways in the Army of describing the faces of people we didn't like, but none of them would do. A couple of fishwives, with a Victorian cabby thrown in, might manage it. My father always used to tell me – '

'But,' interrupted Judy, 'won't you tell us what happened, Colonel?'

'I'm trying to, my dear girl,' went on the Colonel. 'He picked me up by the scruff and shook me like a terrier with a rat. Not that he was like a terrier – good fellows, terriers – insult to compare them with him. Shook me till my jaws rattled. You've never had that, I suppose. These writer fellows are right after all. I'd never have believed it. But my jaws actually rattled. D'you know, while he was doing it, I remember thinking, these writer fellows are right, I thought, the jaws do rattle.'

'Yes, Colonel, but why did he make your jaws rattle?'

'That's what I should like to know. That's what your father will want to know.'

'But was there no reason at all?' asked James.

'My dear fellow – what reason could there be? I'm not much of a chap, I know, but would you say that it was actually a good thing to pick me up and make my jaws rattle? Suspended in the air, I was. I suppose you don't think it matters, my dear fellow, to have your poor old gardener suspended in the air. And d'you know, my dear boy, I didn't even kick the fellow. I remember thinking, while I was hanging there – just after I'd thought that bit about the jaws rattling – you remember, my dear fellow – I remember thinking as I was suspended in the air – I could kick him good and proper now – and then I thought – only foreigners kick – funny how the old school sayings stick in the mind – only foreigners kick – that's what we used to say at school – and then I thought that if I did he might drop me and stamp on me and all that.'

'But how did it all start, Colonel?'

'I'm trying to tell you, my dear boy. It was like this. Now, I say you couldn't have a nicer little innkeeper with a nicer little wife than the Cumberlands, could you now?'

'They're a charming couple.'

'Right. A charming couple, that's what they are. And what happens? It's lucky your father is a good-tempered man – he'd have the military out as well as the police. Shooting and all that. But not here – not in Murrell Keeping. Where had I got to?'

'The Cumberlands.'

'Ah yes. I'd just gone in for my glass of ginger beer and this fellow was there – obviously a foreigner – from Surrey or Sussex or somewhere – might even have been from the north – Yorkshire and all that. Where was I?'

'Yorkshire.'

'Ah, yes – might well have been. Well – apparently he was staying the night at the Bull and the things he was saying to the Cumberlands – they made my blood boil. So I spoke up. "Look here, sir," I said, "it may be the custom in Warwickshire or Dorset" – '

'But, Colonel, what was he saying?'

'I wouldn't repeat it, my dear girl, in front of you. Mark you, it may be the way they talk in Berks Bucks and Oxon – but I wouldn't say it – not even if Mrs Cumberland hadn't been there. If you've a complaint to make, I say, make it civilly – much more effective. I'm sure that's your father's view.'

'What was he complaining about?'

'That wasn't the point, my dear boy. Not the point at all. It was the way he was doing it. So I said: "Now, look here, sir. In Murrell Keeping we keep civil tongues in our heads – ' and that's all I said, my dear fellow, positively all. The next moment I was swinging in the air. And a few moments after that I found myself in the street. And here I am. Mark you, I'm not saying that there wasn't something in what he said – that staircase is a bit awkward for a stranger – if there's no light on. If I wanted to kill a man, I'd ask him there for the night and take the bulb out. But just because he'd had a fright, there's no need to be rude about it, is there? And then, just because I remonstrated with him – ' The Colonel paused. He had seen James and Judy exchanging glances. Naturally he did not appreciate that the same thought had occurred to them both. Could they get Sidney to the Bull for a night, make him drunk, take the bulb out in the hope that he'd fall down the stairs? All Colonel Brain thought was that at last his story had made an impression.

'Ah – I thought that'd shake you, my dear boy,' he went on. 'Now – perhaps – I can see your father.'

'Who was this chap?' asked James.

'No idea.'

'Was he really seven foot with ginger hair?'

'Well, my dear chap, I won't be positive to an inch or two, but he could give you pretty well a foot – and he certainly had ginger hair.'

'Then it wasn't our friend,' said Judy.

'Your friend?' said the Colonel incredulously. 'I'm quite sure no friend of yours would behave like that, my dear girl.'

'Was he drunk?'

'Mad, more like. No, he hadn't even the excuse of being drunk. P'raps he's an escaped lunatic. I'd never thought of that.'

That is, in fact, what the red-haired gentleman was, and long before the colonel had made his complaint to the judge the local constable had been sent for by the Cumberlands and, with the assistance of a number of the younger men in the bar, he had been overpowered. Sidney himself watched the proceedings with interest. He had only arrived after the ejection of Colonel Brain. By then the ginger-haired man had become quite quiet and was sitting peacefully in the bar, when, to Sidney's surprise, a sudden attack was made on him.

'Press gang, I suppose,' he said to himself eventually, 'or have I got my dates wrong? No – it can't be. I would say that these are very strange goings on, very strange indeed. Sidney, my boy, you've had one too many this time.'

Meantime James and Judy, having handed over the colonel to their father, looked at each other for a moment or two without speaking. Eventually James said: 'Well – what about it?'

CHAPTER NINE

Reflections on Murder

It may be a great credit to mankind and a sign of the advance of civilisation that people in the so-called civilised countries do not often even consider killing other people who are in their way, except, of course, on the grand scale during a war. The main exception to this apparent moderation on the part of human beings exists in the case of husbands and wives. If all the husbands and wives who had been poisoned by their mates were exhumed and laid end to end it would surprise and horrify many people to see what a length of the Bayswater Road the bodies would occupy. If the husbands were put on one side and the wives on the other, the husbands would win handsomely. This is because wives have an unfair advantage: they normally do the cooking. But, apart from murder between husband and wife (which goes on regularly and usually undiscovered), premeditated murder for the sake of removing someone who is a nuisance or danger is extremely rare. A few criminals of the lowest class, little different from apes, indulge in it and so occasionally does a megalomaniac. But the ordinary person never even considers the possibility. This may be due to lack of opportunity. As James and Judy appreciated, it is not easy to get someone you want to murder to the edge of a cliff, nor is he or she likely to go on a climbing expedition with you. The danger of using other methods is obvious, and it is only husbands or wives who can use poison with comparative safety. The reason so few poisonings of husbands and wives are detected is mainly the difficulty of diagnosis and the natural reluctance of any doctor to refuse a death certificate. It is not the possible loss of patients through unpopularity that worries doctors but their real dislike of raising what will probably turn out to be unjustified suspicions in the minds of neighbours. Such suspicions, once aroused, seldom disappear. If a post-mortem is ordered by the Coroner the husband or wife of the dead person is always liable to be held suspect by some of the neighbours for ever. The result is that it is a very grave responsibility to refuse a death certificate and doctors do not like taking it. The difficulties of diagnosis and the reluctance of doctors to refuse death certificates are, then, the causes of husbands and wives being in the privileged class of potential undetected murderers. Whether it be lack of opportunity or a high moral standard which keeps other people out of this class, the fact remains that men and women whose death will be a great advantage to someone else are seldom (with the exceptions mentioned) murdered. The clerk waiting for promotion on the death of Jones never even considers pushing him in front of a train. The lover seldom thinks of murdering the husband. Monsieur Vaquier was an exception to this rule. But the clumsy mess he made of it should serve as a warning to other lovers.

Although, therefore, having regard to the gravity of the situation James and Judy did actually discuss the possibility of removing Sidney by killing him and although they made out a strong moral case for doing so, it was not long before they realised that they must find a less objectionable method of achieving their object. At first the simple expedient suggested by Colonel Brain had appealed to them. To hit a man on the head is one thing, but just to take a bulb out and hope seems another. After all, the fellow has a chance of escaping altogether or with only broken bones or bruises. Such a simple thing just to remove a bulb and wait. Discovery most improbable. Nevertheless, the tradition of only killing during a war was too much for them, and, instead, James went to London to consult a barrister friend, Bertram Shuttlebury.

CHAPTER TEN

Sidney Enjoys Himself

'Look,' said James to Bertram, 'what can you do in a case of blackmail other than prosecute, without risking exposure?'

'Is this a play you're writing or are you in a spot yourself?'

'Never mind which. I really want to know. If one can't risk the publicity even of being Mr X, what can one do – except pay and pay? Is there anything?'

'Well, there is, as a matter of fact. It isn't an absolute certainty – nothing can be – but it usually works pretty well.'

'What is it?'

'Just this. A blackmailer will generally agree to anything, provided you pay him. For example, it's his normal habit to say: "If you let me have £50 I'll never trouble you again." Then, of course, two months later he comes along and says the same thing. And so on.'

'Where is this leading to?'

'I'll tell you. If you can get a blackmailer to enter into an agreement, preferably in writing, by which in return for a certain sum he promises never to speak or write to you again directly or indirectly and never to publish to anyone the thing you're frightened of his publishing, you can normally enforce that agreement without any publicity.'

'How?'

'Well, assume you pay him the money and he signs the agreement and then comes back and asks for more. As soon as he does so you issue a writ in the Queen's Bench Division and ask for an injunction to restrain him from doing any of the things he's promised not to do. A judge will usually grant such an injunction pending the trial of the action. It can do the defendant no harm. If he breaks it, he goes to prison. If he doesn't break it, you're all right.'

'But surely there's publicity attached to the granting of the injunction?'

'None at all. In the Queen's Bench Division it's all done privately before what we call a judge in chambers. Of course, it's only a temporary injunction pending the trial of the action. But, from the blackmailer's point of view, there's no point in bringing the action to trial, as the only result from his point of view is that he'd be likely to be charged with blackmail. Accordingly, in most cases he agrees to a permanent order and that's the end of the affair. As I've said, it isn't a one hundred per cent certainty, but usually it works.'

'Could you write out the sort of thing one should get him to sign?'

'Certainly. If you're really serious, I'll do it now.'

In consequence, James came back from London with an agreement for Sidney to sign. He and Judy decided to say nothing to their father until after it was signed. By pooling their resources they had managed to raise £200 and they at once wired to Sidney inviting him to stay the night at the Bull and stating that they hoped to be able to come to some suitable arrangement with him.

'I'm not such a fool after all,' he said. 'I would say that I am very far from being a fool. A knave if you like. But a fool? No. Definitely not. Where the hell's my breakfast?'

While James and Judy were waiting for their meeting with Sidney, and Sidney was calculating how much to ask for in the first instance, Mr Justice Beverley had decided to enlist the help of Scotland Yard. He was determined not to pay Sidney and he did not want to prosecute. The latter would mean his resignation, even if his name were theoretically anonymous. Even a nonentity called Mr X has to appear in court and will probably be recognised by some people, but a well-known man can never retain anonymity in such circumstances. He did not propose to pay Sidney, first because he would not yield to threats on principle and secondly because he knew he would not be able to keep it up. So he decided to see what help the police could give him. He asked to see Bernard Kent. Kent was naturally pleased to see his future father-in-law, but slightly apprehensive in case the judge had something against him.

'How are you, Bernard?' said the judge. 'Nice of you to see me without notice.'

'Not at all, judge. I do hope it's all right about Judy and me.'

'I'm delighted. I hope you'll both be very happy.'

'Thank you very much. I must say it's a bit of a relief. When your name was given to me I thought you might have come to complain that I hadn't asked you first.'

'I'm not as out-of-date as all that,' said the judge. 'No, I'm afraid I've come to ask for some help.'

He then told Bernard the whole story.

'Hanging's too good for him,' said Bernard when the judge had finished.

'I dare say, but that doesn't help me. It may be that I ought never to have accepted a judgeship. But it's too late to think of that now. It may be that I ought to resign now. Well – I'm not going to if I can help it. I must do another year first, if it's humanly possible. I thought that a couple of your chaps might be able to frighten him off. He's well known to some of your departments. I don't know whether he's done this sort of thing before, but he's an old customer of yours. A few words from a determined police officer might do the trick.'

So Bernard Kent arranged for two important CID officers to find Mr Sidney York and give him the necessary warning. It was, therefore, not long after Sidney had received the telegram from James that he was told that there were two gentlemen to see him.

'What the hell can they want?' he said. 'Ask them their business.'

He was told that they were police officers. And he at once went downstairs. They said who they were.

'Come in, gentlemen,' he said. 'What can I do for you?'

'Now look,' said Deputy Commander Trew, 'we look upon blackmail as worse than murder.'

'Agreed,' said Sidney. 'Moral murder it's called. You haven't come all the way from Scotland Yard to tell me that, I hope. Even though I assume you haven't had to walk.'

'You recently called on Sir John Beverley, the High Court judge.'

'To be sure, I did. What's funny about that? Now, if a High Court judge called on me, that would be odd. It's usually his Clerk or whatever it is who calls on me and then it's just to ask if I have anything to say why sentence should not be passed on me according to law. But why remind me of such things? I've turned over a new leaf, gentlemen. Going straight, it's called – well, as straight as that bottle of whisky will allow me. Forgive me for not offering you one, but it's scarce – well – too scarce anyway.'

'Don't try to be funny. York,' said the Deputy Commander. 'You haven't had more than five years up to now. You'd get a lifer for blackmail. And you'll get no whisky in gaol.'

'Well – I'm not so sure of that really. It's a necessity for me now. I'd die without it. They'd give it to me as a medicine. Oh – yes – I shall die of it too, no doubt. But I was forgetting, you said something about blackmail. I can't think what you're talking about. Never done such a thing in my life.'

'You went to Sir John Beverley and threatened to sell an article to the Clarion if he didn't pay you not to.'

'You amaze me, honestly you do. There must be some horrible mistake.'

'There's no mistake at all.'

'But there must be. Because, if I'd done that, I should be in custody already. You can't imagine a High Court judge letting me get away with that.'

The Deputy Commander hesitated. The interview was getting a little out of hand. Sidney, seeing from the hesitation that he was on firm ground, pressed home his advantage. 'And then, again, if I may say so, you'd have come here to arrest me if I'd really done a thing like that. It's not like careless driving or obstruction where you may give a chap a warning first. You don't warn people for blackmail. Might just as well warn them for murder. "Now, Mr Jones, if you go killing any more people, we shall take a very serious view of the matter, a very serious view indeed." But do tell me, joking apart, what is this all about? It isn't April the first or anything is it?'

'I warn you, York,' said the Deputy Commander, 'that if any article appears in the Clarion about Sir John Beverley, you'll be prosecuted for blackmail.'

'Do, please, say that again. I can hardly believe my ears.'

The Deputy Commander repeated it.

'But, Commander Trew, I'm sure you'll forgive me, but that in itself sounds very like blackmail to me. Suppose I were a journalist trying to earn an honest living and then you come and threaten me to prevent me from earning it – isn't that blackmail itself – very like it, I should say, very like it indeed.'

'You may think you're very clever, York,' said the Deputy Commander, keeping his end up as best he could, 'but you're riding for a very heavy fall, I assure you.'

'I wish you wouldn't talk in metaphors, Commander Trew. What I can't understand is why, if I've done all these dreadful things – and I assure you I haven't – word of honour – what I can't understand is why you don't arrest me now. Mark you, I'm delighted that you don't. Do tell me – in confidence, of course, you know you can trust me – why don't you?'

'I'm not here to answer your questions,' said the Deputy Commander lamely.

'Of course not. But I must say it's a bit thick to tell a chap he's guilty of blackmail, that you can prove it by the evidence of a High Court judge – he'd be bound to be believed, wouldn't he – even if he weren't on oath – and then just to threaten me. I'm sure it's against the judges' rules. You haven't a copy of them on you, I suppose?'

The Deputy Commander ignored the remark and, unpleasant though he found it to have his tail twisted by Sidney, he decided that, at any rate, he had better get as much evidence as possible.

'You were in the 1914 war with Sir John, were you not?' he asked.

'I was, indeed. I must say we were better friends then than we are now. We've gone rather different ways, I'm afraid.'

'Were you court martialled for an offence concerning a woman?'

'Indeed I was. No doubt you know, too, that I was acquitted. I haven't always been as fortunate since.'

'Did Sir John give evidence for you?'

'He did, indeed. As a matter of fact, he happened to be with me at the time I was supposed to be with the young lady. It was lucky for me. What you call an alibi, Commander Trew, but I don't have to teach you these technical terms.'

'Did you give evidence yourself?'

'I certainly did.'

'Denying the charge?'

'Of course.'

'Was the evidence true?'

'What a question. Naturally. Johnny boy – forgive me – that's what I used to call him – he said the same as me.'

Sidney paused for a moment. 'Commander Trew, a horrible thought has just occurred to me. Do relieve my mind of it. You seem, from your manner, to be suggesting that my evidence was untrue. Well, it was true, as a matter of fact, but, if it wasn't, neither was Johnny boy's. What a horrible thought. You wouldn't suggest that a High Court judge had committed perjury, would you – even all those years ago.'

'Well – as he didn't,' said the Deputy Commander, 'there won't be any articles in the *Clarion* saying that he did.'

'I should be most surprised if there were,' said Sidney. 'But I really don't know why you should expect me to answer for what appears in the newspapers. That does seem to be going a bit far. And they do make mistakes sometimes, you know. I hope you wouldn't blame me if they made one this time.'

'We should not only blame you, but you would be charged with blackmail.'

'There you go again. I simply don't understand. As I understand the word – correct me if I'm wrong – blackmail means demanding money with menaces. Either I've done that already – in which case you have a plain duty to arrest me – I'll come quietly, I assure you – as you probably know – I always do – or I haven't done it already. If I haven't done it already, I can't see why, if I happened to sell an article to the *Clarion*, I should be guilty of a crime. It isn't yet a crime to write for the newspapers, is it? Unless, of course, it's libellous.'

The Deputy Commander thought he saw an opening there. 'Well – if the article said that Sir John had committed perjury when he hadn't, it would be libellous.'

'So it would – Commander Trew – so it would. And a very serious libel, too, I should say. So you mean I should be prosecuted for libel – not blackmail – do you? You mixed up the offences perhaps. But you can hardly be blamed for that, can you? Dealing with all the crimes you're concerned with, I'm surprised you don't make more mistakes.'

'There's no need to be insolent, York. You know quite well what I mean. You won't get another warning.'

'Well, I should hope not, Commander Trew, if it's anything like this one. I have had to complain once or twice about warnings given before I made a statement, but they were nothing to this. You seem to be compounding a felony and committing one all at the same time. Which, if I may say so, is bad for a Deputy Commander. I would say it was very bad indeed. And that reminds me. I do feel extremely honoured at having such distinguished guests. I've never had more than an inspector before. Oh – yes – once – my memory's not as good as it was – I did once have a superintendent. I can't think why. It was quite a simple case. Now, is there anything more I can do for you, gentlemen? If not, perhaps you'd excuse me? I feel it's time to get on with the day's drinking – and, as I said before, I shan't persuade you to join me.'

As soon as the officers had gone, Sidney called for Martha.

'Old girl,' he said, 'they've got the wind up. Got it badly. If we play our cards right, we're on a sitter. Where's that telegram? I'll go down tonight. Go and buy yourself a new nightdress. I want you to look nice when I come back. And, my dear sweet Martha, I'll give you hell if you don't – and perhaps even if you do. Now, give me a drink.'

The only thing the Deputy Commander said to his companion on his way back to Scotland Yard was: 'I'd like to wring his ruddy neck.'

There was, in fact, almost unanimity that Sidney ought to be put out of the way, but the sanctity of human life or the lack of opportunity – according to which view is taken of the matter – stood him in good stead, though he himself would have been the first to admit that hanging was too good for him.

'I would say,' he would probably have said, if the subject had been broached, 'I would say that it would be very much too good. Where's my breakfast?'

CHAPTER ELEVEN

The End of Sidney

Mr and Mrs Cumberland were, as Colonel Brain had said, a charming couple. He was over seventy, and she was some years younger. On the day on which Sidney was to come for the night, Mrs Cumberland was chatting to her husband as he put in a new switch in the lounge so that the light over the dangerous stairs could be operated from below. The ginger-headed man had been a lunatic, but his complaint had been far from unreasonable. It was his manner of making it that was objected to. The stairs themselves were a death-trap without a light. They were steep and ended up at the bottom with a solid oak door opening on to the kitchen. Colonel Brain's suggested method of killing someone was quite one of his better ideas. Anyone falling down the stairs would have an excellent chance of breaking his neck or his skull if the door at the bottom of the staircase was closed.

'Well,' said Mr Cumberland, 'I don't know why the cheaper one wasn't good enough for you. And this is more to clean.'

'If a thing's worth doing, it's worth doing well. But does it work? That's the chief thing.'

Mr Cumberland pressed the switch, and the light went on upstairs.

'There,' he said. 'And you wanted to waste money on an electrician. I told you I could do it.'

'Not bad,' said his wife, 'but, while you're about it, you might put in a stronger bulb upstairs.'

'It's a twenty-five.'

'It's too dim.'

'But they'll leave it on all night.'

'I can't help that. You want a forty at least. Change it with the one in the lavatory.'

'All right, if you insist, but think of the money wasted just because people can't remember to press a switch.'

'This one's meant to be left on – and, anyway, you can't talk about people being forgetful. You get worse every day.'

'That's true enough,' said Mr Cumberland. 'Which reminds me. Oh – dear – oh dear. I never sent that telegram for the vicar.' He started to feel in his pockets.

'Now, where could it be, I wonder? I promised I wouldn't forget. What shall I say to him?'

'Was that the wire to his daughter up north?' asked Mrs Cumberland.

'That's the one. I can't even find it.'

'That's not surprising. You gave it to me and I sent it.'

'Did I really? Well – that's a bit of luck. You're sure?'

'Yes, don't you remember – you were serving at the time?'

'No, can't remember at all. That's bad, that. I'd have sworn I'd still got it in my pocket. What'll I forget next, I wonder?'

'But the way you looked at Elsie, I sometimes thought you'd forgotten you were married to me.'

'Elsie? Elsie? Who's she?'

'You know perfectly well who Elsie is. Our last barmaid.'

'That's the one. Where is she?'

'She left last week.'

'Pity. Lovely hair she had. It would have come below her knees I should think.'

'That one left six months ago – and I hope you never saw it there.'

'No – my dear. Just wishful thinking. All right – I'll go and change the lamp for you. You see, I haven't forgotten that yet.' He went up the stairs and took the lamp out and came down with it in his hand. As he was nearing the bottom of the stairs he stopped. 'Bother,' he said. 'I forgot to put that bet on for the colonel. Saucy Sue, wasn't it? A shilling each way.'

'The colonel doesn't bet. It must have been for someone else.'

'No – it was for the colonel. I remember him saying he didn't bet. Now, what have I said? Something wrong there. No, I remember, it was for old Lumsden.'

'He's been dead for the last three years.'

'Of course he has. Well – I'm glad I remembered it wasn't for the colonel. That's something. P'raps I'm improving.'

'Well – I'm going back to the bar. Don't forget to make that bill out for the Temples before you do anything else.'

'It's the next thing I'll do.'

Mrs Cumberland went back to the bar, and her husband went to the lavatory and changed the bulb. He came back to the lounge and was starting to go up the stairs when he suddenly stopped. What was it his wife had told him to do? He scratched his head, came down a stair or two, then went up again, then came down.

'What was it, now?' he said aloud. Suddenly his face lighted up, and he came down into the lounge and walked confidently towards a desk, the lamp still in his hand. But, as he got nearer to the desk, his face clouded over again. He stood for a moment by the desk, thinking.

'For the life of me,' he said. Suddenly he had a thought, he put the lamp bulb in a bowl on a table and walked confidently towards the light switch. He looked at it for a moment as though disappointed that it seemed to be in order. Then he had a brilliant idea. He switched it on. Nothing happened. 'Now, what on earth – ' he began, when he was interrupted by James coming in. They started chatting and within a minute or two all thoughts of the bet on Saucy Sue, the bill for the Temples and the electric light bulb had disappeared.

'Mr Cumberland,' said James eventually, 'Judy and I are seeing a chap on business here tonight. It's rather important and confidential. Would it be possible for you to keep people out of the lounge as much as possible?'

'Certainly. When's he coming?'

'Any moment now, as a matter of fact. We're going to have a couple of drinks in the bar with him first. He's staying the night here. That's what he said in his wire, anyway.'

'No use telling me his name – simply can't remember names. But, of course, we'll keep the lounge clear for you. How long do you want it for?'

'Only about half an hour or so, I should say.'

Not long afterwards Sidney was met at the station by James and Judy.

'A reception committee?' he said. 'How nice. I should say most thoughtful, very thoughtful indeed.'

'This is my sister,' said James.

'How d'you do? This is a privilege. I really am going to enjoy myself. If I may say so, if your father's judgments are as beautiful as his daughter, they must be very well received, and never appealed against.'

They walked to the Bull, James carrying Sidney's small attaché case containing only a pair of pyjamas, shaving and washing things.

'Always travel light,' he said. 'For one thing, I hate carrying things. For another, there's less to lose.'

On arrival at the Bull, Sidney signed the visitors' book and was told where his room was. He decided to accept the offer of a drink before going to it. They went into the private bar and, after he had had four very large whiskies, James and Judy decided that he was in a sufficiently benevolent mood to approach, and they took him into the lounge and sat next to him on the sofa.

'Well,' said Sidney, a little thickly, 'this is great fun. I said to myself on the way – "This is going to be very pleasurable, I should say this is going to be very pleasurable indeed." How right I was. I'll tell you another thing I said. Would you like to know?'

'What was it?' said Judy.

'I said to myself – you'll be thinking I talk rather a lot to myself – quite right, I do – the great advantage is I don't answer back – or, if I do, I'm always polite to myself – never bite my head off – unless of course, I've been really rude to myself – but, even then, I tick myself off in the nicest possible way – make myself feel rather a cad – you shouldn't have said that to yourself. I say, you really shouldn't. That wasn't thoughtful, was it? Come on, own up, it wasn't thoughtful. Eventually I'll make myself answer – takes quite a bit of doing – I can be dreadfully stubborn, but I usually persuade myself in the end and we go on the best of friends. You'll gather I rather like myself. Now, where had I got to? Oh yes – I said to myself – "Now, I wonder what it is he wants to see me about?" And, for once, I didn't get any reply. Usually I find myself most communicative, even talkative. But this time I couldn't get

115

a word out of myself. I repeated the question. "What does he want?" I said. But the only answer was the noise of the train – and the man breathing opposite to me. So perhaps, now I'm here, you could enlighten me.'

'We've got an agreement here we thought you might be prepared to make with us.'

'Dear me. How interesting. An agreement. What's it all about? Do I get anything out of it?'

'Oh, yes, you do.'

'That sounds a nice agreement, I must say. How much would you say I get out of it?'

'Well – it all depends on how much you want.'

'Oh – that will never do. My wants are like the curiosity of the elephant's child – d'you remember what it was?'

'Can you give us an idea? We're not well off, you know, but we'll try to meet you.'

'How very kind. But, you know, I was once given a word of advice by a businessman – a very wise old bird he was – he went to gaol in the end – but that really wasn't his fault – what he said was: "Never start the bidding. Make the other fellow begin. Of course, he'll start much too low, but that doesn't matter. You can always push him up. But the tragic thing is, if you start, you may mention a figure which is below the one he was prepared to go to. That really is tragedy. Romeo and Juliet isn't in it." So, you see, I'd like you to begin. I'm all attention. Or perhaps I could have another drink first. As you probably realise, I have a perpetual thirst. It's a delightful thing to have – provided you've the means of slaking it. It is a bit of a problem now with whisky at its present price.'

James fetched another drink for Sidney and decided that he'd better make some kind of an offer.

'Would £50 be any use to you?' he asked.

'£50?' said Sidney. 'It would be most useful. Are you really offering to give me £50? That is most kind. I would say that it was very kind indeed.'

There was a pause. Neither James nor Judy knew quite what to make of this apparent acceptance of their first offer.

'Well,' said Sidney, 'is that all you asked me to come here for? Don't think I'm complaining. On the contrary, I think it charming. You want to give me £50. And I may tell you I shall be delighted to accept it. Let's have another drink on the strength of it. You don't happen to have the money with you?'

'I do as a matter of fact.'

'How very thoughtful. I hope it's in pound notes. So much easier to change than fivers. They used to make you put your name and address on fivers. Not that I mind people knowing my name and address, but you never know into whose hands it may get. Quite undesirable people sometimes. Race gangs and so on. I just don't like the idea of their having my name and address. Of course, it's true they could turn your name up in the telephone book, but that's different somehow. Yes, pound notes are much more convenient. You really are most considerate.' He paused and then: 'There's nothing you want out of me in return, I suppose? It's just a free gift?'

'Well, as a matter of fact we should like you to sign this agreement – just as a matter of form, you know.'

'Oh – dear – I don't like those words "just as a matter of form." P'raps it's because I've used them myself occasionally. They savour of the tally man persuading the housewife to sign a most inequitable contract. What a pity you said that. I hope it's not going to spoil the evening.'

'It's only quite a simple agreement really.'

'Well – if that's all it is, why bother?'

'I think it's only reasonable we should have something for our £50.'

'Oh dear – you have disappointed me. I thought you were just being nice. But it's the same the world over. Something for nothing – it just doesn't exist. But I suppose I shouldn't grumble – I've never given something for nothing yet – not since I reached years of discretion anyway.'

There was a silence for a few seconds.

'If you'd sign it,' said James, 'we might manage a little over the £50.'

'An auction?' said Sidney. 'That's just what I like. Great fun. Shall I play the auctioneer? Then you two had better be the bidders. Let me see. Yes, I've got it. You' – and he pointed to James – 'are Mr Anstruther – Nicholas Anstruther – you very much want the next item – you're prepared to go quite a long way – d'you follow me? – you've set your heart on it. And you're' – and he pointed to Judy – 'you're Miss – Miss Luscious Lovely – what charming legs you've got, if I may so – but that's another story, I suppose. Well – you want this next item too – very badly. So that'll keep the bidding bright and cheerful. Good – are we ready? Now, ladies and gentlemen, I have here a most valuable manuscript – and the author will sign it. I'm authorited – authorited – I'm credibly informed that it is the only copy in existence. It's only by a series of fortunate coincidences that I'm enabled to offer it. The owner is going abroad. He doesn't like parting with it at all – indeed, I had to exercise all my powers of persuasion to get him to do so – but, if he gets a high enough offer, he'll take it. I'm afraid there's a pretty substantial reserve. I'll tell you when we reach it. Now, will someone open the bidding? Come along now. Don't be nervous. Someone's got to begin. What about you, sir? I couldn't quite hear – £50? Thank you very much, sir – £50 I'm bid by the gentleman over there – but it's giving it away at that – madam, you're not going to let it go for nothing – £60? Thank you very much. £60. It's against you, sir – £65? Thank you. £70, madam?'

'Look here – let's stop this nonsense,' said James. 'We'll pay £100.'

'That's very generous – but I was just enjoying myself. Don't spoil my fun. I don't get so much nowadays. We'll go on from there then, shall we? It's against the lady with the lovely legs. £105? Thank you very much, madam. Now, sir, don't be beaten by a lady. But what about another drink? This is thirsty work.'

'I'll get you one.'

While James was getting the drink, Sidney turned his drunken and increasingly amorous eyes on Judy. 'Nice fellow, your brother, inviting me down here. But I wish he'd leave us alone for a bit. I could think of quite a lot to say to you.' He put his hand on Judy's knee and she moved quickly away.

'That's all right,' said Sidney. 'I like 'em frisky. Ever tried to catch a colt? Great fun it is when they've a sense of humour. Some of them must have, you know. They wait till you're almost up to them with a twinkle in their eye – and then, just as you think you've got them – ' Sidney paused and raised his hand. 'Now, wait for it,' he added, as Judy got up. 'Then, just as you get to them, up go their legs and they're off and away. Just like you. Only you didn't do the leg part very well. Shall we try again? D'you know, a sudden thought has just occurred to me. D'you know what it is?'

Judy said nothing.

'Come on, have a guess. D'you know what it is? Now, don't sulk. I can't stand sulky people. And, if you want to do business with me, you'll have to go my way about it. Come on, give me a smile. That'd be something to go on with. You're putting ideas into my head, d'you see? That's a dangerous thing to do. I would say it was very dangerous indeed.' James returned with the drink. Sidney drank half of it at once. 'So you want me to sign something, do you, in exchange for – what was it – £150 or £200? Shocking memory I've got for figures – not bad for other things, but hopeless at figures.'

'All right,' said James. 'We'll go to £200, if you'll sign this agreement.'

'You said that too quickly,' said Sidney. 'That means you'll go higher.'

'It doesn't. That's our utmost limit.'

'Well – I must admit that you said that very convincingly. You're coming on a bit. Now shall I tell you something?'

He waited. 'Well – shall I?'

'What is it?'

'Just this. I am well aware that you have been filling me up with whisky in the hope that I'd sign your silly agreement. Well, that's all right. I like the process.' He finished the remainder of his drink and went on: 'But let me tell you that drunk or sober I sign nothing – nothing. I never did like signing things and I'm not starting now.'

'You won't get a penny unless you do,' said James, boldly.

'Oh – don't get nasty, please,' said Sidney. 'Don't spoil the party. Talking of which, what about another?' James looked despairingly at Judy and went out with the empty glass.

'Well – you see – I'm doing everything you wanted – coming over here – drinking as fast as I can – as much as I can – except just the one little thing – my signature. I must admit, though, that I'm feeling nice and fuddled. Now's really the time to get me to sign. Why not try and wheedle me? I should enjoy that and you never know what might happen. Come on, have a try. If you wait much longer, I shall be too drunk to write at all – even if you guided my hand. That's an idea – if you guided my hand – I might – I only said "might" – sign the thing. Now, where is it? Come on, let's have it.' Judy handed him the agreement which James had left on the table. Sidney pretended to read it.

'Can't make head or tail of it,' he said eventually. 'But where's my pen? Ah – here it is. Now, you come over here and see what happens. Come along now. What are you waiting for? Really, this is absurd. It's I who am wheedling you instead of the other way about.'

Eventually Judy decided that there was no harm in trying. The man was very drunk and she could always call for help if necessary. She went over to the sofa and brought a small table up to it for Sidney to write on.

'That's better,' he said. 'Come along and give me your hand – your lovely cool hand. Come on now, you're not frightened of a drunken old wreck like me – you could knock me over with a push. Now, here's the agreement. You put your hand on mine and we'll see what happens.' Judy gave him her hand.

'That's beautiful. It really is. Now, what shall I write?'

'Just your name.'

'Now – let me see – what is it at the moment?'

'Sidney York.'

'That's it, is it? But d'you think that'd be all right? I've got so many other names. Would it be legal, d'you think?'

'I've no idea. But if that's what it says at the top, I should think it would do.'

'Quite a little lawyer. Shouldn't mind having a lawyer like you. I'd have a lot of conferences. Now d'you think you could put a little more pressure on my hand? I'm finding it very heavy work. Go on, harder than that. That's better. It's actually beginning to move. Now, what do I put? I remember.' He started to spell out the name. 'S-I-D-N-E-Y – that's Sidney. Now – Y-O-R-K – that's York. The whole – Sidney York. What a pity there wasn't any ink in the pen. It hasn't even made a mark. What a shame. And I really did enjoy it. Ah, this'll cheer me up a bit. Why don't you have one?' James had come back with Sidney's drink.

'I think I will,' said Judy. 'Could you get me a gin and French? This is hopeless.'

'Oh – not hopeless. Never give up. I've got some more ideas already. Thank goodness he's gone. Now, fill my pen for me, there's a good girl. That's right. Now, come over here and sit nice and close. I won't touch you. Don't you trust me? You can, you know. D'you know why? Because I didn't say "I promise." That was the one good thing my mother taught me. She never made me say "I promise" or "honour bright" or anything of that sort. You know the way parents do. "Have you taken any jam?" "No." "Honour bright?" In other words, the mere word isn't accepted – result – the mere word doesn't mean anything. Now, I was brought up to keep my word. It's true I may not always do so, but saying "promise" or "cross my heart" or "swear" won't make me any more likely to do so.'

Judy's patience was now quite exhausted. 'If you're not too drunk to understand plain English – '

'I say – that's too bad,' interrupted Sidney. 'You're making me drunk. It doesn't lie in your mouth to say things like that.'

'Are you going to sign this agreement or not and how much d'you want for doing so?'

'It's no use trying to rush me, my dear girl. Can't you see I'm enjoying myself? Don't often get the chance of a tête-a-tête with a judge's daughter – even though your tiresome brother does keep interrupting. Can't you send him away or something – after he's brought the next drink, I mean?'

'I'm quite sure you're enjoying playing with us. I shouldn't mind going on if I thought you'd sign the thing in the end.'

'Now, that's one of the most sensible things you've said so far. All right – I will sign the thing in the end. When I've had my bit of fun. That's fair enough, isn't it?'

James came back with the drinks.

'Thanks, my boy,' said Sidney. 'I was just saying that I will sign your bit of paper – after I've had my bit of fun.'

'Meaning?'

'Just what I say. My bit of fun. A couple of hundred pounds as well, of course. There isn't so much fun in the world for a chap like me. So when I see a chance, I've got to take it.'

'What d'you want us to do then? Tell you funny stories?' Sidney tried to look pained, but the muscles of his face did not respond easily owing to the amount of drink he had taken.

'That's being stupid, my dear boy – I would say it was being very stupid indeed. Now, I tell you what. I'll make a bargain with you. If you'll come up to my room with me – not you, you fool – you, I mean – nothing improper, of course – if you'll come up to my room and guide my hand with yours – so delightfully cool it was – we haven't told him yet about our first try – and bring £200 with you – you can leave it on the mantelpiece – I'll sign your silly little bit of nonsense. Now, what could be fairer than that? Now don't try and talk to each other with your eyes. Go into a huddle in the corner, I shan't listen.'

James and Judy took his advice. 'I'm sure he's just playing with us. I don't believe he'll sign the thing for a moment,' said Judy.

'Well, that's that,' said James.

'All the same,' said Judy, 'he's so drunk I might get him to sign it. There's no danger of any funny business. He hasn't the strength of a child in this condition. And, if there were any trouble, I'd give a yell. I think it's worth having a final go. And don't worry – if it takes some time. After all, it's our only chance.'

They talked it over for another minute before deciding to agree to Sidney's suggestion.

'Look,' said Sidney, 'don't be all night. I shall be asleep if you keep me waiting much longer.'

'All right,' said Judy. 'I'll come up with you.'

'That's my darling,' said Sidney. 'That's the nicest thing I've heard for years. Now, you run along up first – I'll just have another quick one first. My room's number one. Shouldn't have remembered it otherwise. You'll find it beautifully tidy – at least I hope so – as I haven't been there yet. Make yourself at home. I shan't keep you waiting long. Just a small stag party with your brother first.'

Judy went upstairs. After she had been gone a short time, James went up after her. He wasn't happy about the whole thing – but Judy persuaded him to go down again. As soon as he came down, he spoke to Sidney. 'Now, look – ' he began, but Sidney interrupted him.

'Don't say it, my dear boy. Please don't. Or shall I say it for you? If I touch a hair of her head, you'll kill me with your bare hands. That right? Well, take my advice and don't do any such thing. First of all, they'd hang you – which would be a bad thing, wouldn't it – I would say that it would be very bad indeed. To go on with, everyone would want to know what it was all about. And things might get into the papers. That wouldn't do your father or mother any good, would it? When you've a decision to make, my dear boy, act like an accountant and draw up a balance sheet first. I'll draw one for you. Two, in fact. Balance sheet A: You come and kill me. Debit side: exit the Beverley family *en masse*, you via the hangman. Credit side: I miss my bit of fun. Hardly seems to balance, does it? Now, look at balance sheet B. You don't come up – or kill me. Debit side: I have my bit of fun. Credit side: I sign your agreement and the Beverleys live happily ever after. That's a better picture, isn't it?'

'You can talk as much as you like,' said James, 'but when I say "I warn you," I mean it.'

'Of course there's a third possibility,' went on Sidney. 'Silly of me not to think of it. I ought really to have mentioned it first. You might just come and knock me about. Now, I do want to warn you as a friend not to do anything silly like that. Because that would be so bad for you all. You'd have been much better advised never to invite me here than do that. I don't suppose you'd be prosecuted – a brother going to the rescue of his sister – even if he went a bit too far would have too strong a case – but a lot of things would certainly come out in the papers then – and the object of this exercise is to prevent that, isn't it? So do be sensible. Not that it matters much to me. In my present condition I should hardly feel it. Well, I think I might go up now, don't you? Shouldn't keep a lady waiting. I'll ring if I want you.'

Sidney got up and started, with some difficulty and very slowly, to go up the stairs. He found it quite an effort. As he went up, he tried to hum the Lohengrin Wedding March, but his difficulty in breathing made it almost unrecognisable. Eventually he reached the top and paused to get some breath. After about half a minute's wait he started slowly along the corridor, after calling down to James: 'Or do you prefer the Mendelssohn?'

James was still not at all happy about it, but it did seem that Judy could come to no harm. She was quite a strong young woman and even a weaker person should have been able to cope quite comfortably with Sidney in that condition. All the same, he didn't like it. He was listening intently for the slightest sound, when Colonel Brain came in.

'There you are, my dear fellow. And the party's over, I see. I told old Cumberland you wouldn't mind my butting in. He wanted to keep me out. Sure I'm not in the way?'

'Oh – no – that's all right,' said James, not very happily.

'It's about that ginger pop you owe me, my dear boy. I've a terrible thirst and I thought I might as well have it now.'

'Oh – yes – of course – I'd forgotten, Colonel. Do go and have it. Would you forgive me not joining you for the moment? I'll be in a little later.'

'Well – certainly, my dear fellow. But can't I have it here with you? Much more friendly. I ought really to be standing you one. I'm sure you missed that putt on purpose.'

'No, really, Colonel,' said James. He couldn't make out why he hadn't heard the door upstairs open and close. But there hadn't been a sound since Sidney had passed out of his view along the corridor. The silence was uncanny.

'Well – I'll go and fetch it and bring it here – if that's all right.'

'Oh – yes – certainly – Colonel – or – perhaps – I wonder if you'd think me very rude if I said I'd join you in the bar? I want to have a word with Judy first.'

'Oh – where's she?'

'Powdering her nose, I think.'

'Very well, my dear boy.' The colonel started to go out, when he noticed James' curious expression. 'What's the matter, my dear boy? You look as though you were listening for something.'

At that moment Mr Cumberland came in. 'Sorry to interrupt,' he said, 'but there's a message from your father. He wants you to go home at once. Rather important, it sounded.'

'Oh – thank you,' said James. Perhaps the colonel and Mr Cumberland coming in had prevented him from hearing the door closing. But it was very strange. And then there was a sound. There was no doubt what it was. Someone had fallen down the stairs – and very heavily too. There was a bump at the end of the fall.

'The light,' said the colonel. 'It's not on.'

Mr Cumberland ran to the switch and turned it on. 'The bulb must have gone. I only put it in this evening. It worked all right then. But come along quick, someone must have been hurt.'

James and Colonel Brain followed Mr Cumberland out of the lounge and into the kitchen. They opened the door to the stairs, and Sidney fell in. He was obviously dead.

'Poor fellow,' said Colonel Brain.

Meanwhile, Judy, having heard the crash, rushed down into the lounge. She was going out, when Mr Cumberland came in.

'No, don't come, please. It's too late. He's dead.'

'Dead?'

'I'm afraid so. But it's that lamp again. It must have gone.'

He went straight upstairs. Judy moved nervously about the lounge. She had nothing to be nervous about, and, thank God, he was dead, but sudden death, except in a war, is usually disturbing. When James first came into the lounge, he had put his hat casually into the bowl where Mr Cumberland had left the lamp. Judy picked it up, for no particular reason – and then saw the lamp underneath. Almost at the same moment, she heard Mr Cumberland shout out: 'The bulb's gone. Someone's taken it out.' In a split second she remembered how James had come to her before Sidney did. She did not remember one way or the other whether the lamp was on when she went up. She was so used to the place that she didn't need it. She hesitated for a moment and then, as she heard Mr Cumberland coming down the stairs, she slipped it into her bag.

'It's extraordinary. Who on earth could have taken it out? I put it there myself. Well, it's too late now. The poor chap's dead. Must have broken his neck. Was he a great friend of yours?'

CHAPTER TWELVE

The Lamp Bulb

Judy sat down in a chair. 'D'you think I could have a drink?' she said.

'Of course. I'll get one at once. Brandy?'

'I do feel a bit faint. The shock, you know. No – he wasn't a friend.'

At that moment Colonel Brain came in. 'Poor fellow,' he said. 'Glad you didn't see him, Judy. Wouldn't have done you any good. Or him either, poor chap. Only one place for him, I'm afraid. But let's talk about something pleasant.'

'I don't feel like talking much at all, I'm afraid. Where's James?'

'He'll be here in a moment, but I expect he's forgotten. Your father wants him. Just telephoned. Ah – this'll do you good.' Mr Cumberland had come in with some drinks.

'No, not for me, thank you. Not even in a crisis. Never have. But you down that, my dear girl, and you'll feel better.'

Judy sipped the brandy. She felt very weak at the knees. It had all happened so quickly. And it was so much that had happened. James put his head round the door.

'You all right, old girl? I've got to get back to father.'

129

'I'll be OK in a moment,' said Judy, making an effort. 'You go on.'

'Right. You wait here and I'll come back and fetch you.' James went out with the colonel. As soon as he'd gone, Judy collapsed, and Mr Cumberland called for his wife, who was soon on the scene.

Then the colonel came hurrying in. 'He wants the ignition key. It's in her bag,' he said. 'Ah – there it is. I'll take it to him and bring it back. Got ticked off last time for feeling in a lady's handbag.'

The colonel took the bag to James. 'Here you are, my dear boy.'

'Thanks, colonel,' began James, and then, feeling for the key, found the lamp.

'What's the matter?' said the colonel. 'Pricked yourself or something?'

'Yes,' said James. 'Look, I must fly.' He found the ignition key, shut the bag and started the car.

'I'll take it back to her,' said the colonel. But James, shouting something unintelligible, had driven off, taking the bag with him.

'It's the shock, I suppose,' said the colonel to himself, 'but, after all, he was in the Army. Seems to be in a panic and all that. Oh well – these young men. It was different when I failed the Staff College.' He went back to the lounge, where Judy was recovering. It was only a hysterical faint, for which she may reasonably be excused. Relief, at the sudden death of a man who was likely to wreck her parents' lives, coupled with the normal amount of shock the sudden death of anyone would be likely to cause, was followed almost immediately by the belief that her brother was the cause of the man's death. The combination was too much for her and she had passed out for a minute or two.

'Where's my bag?' she eventually asked.

'Jimmy took it with him,' said the colonel. 'As a matter of fact, I offered to bring it back to you – I'd taken it for him to get the ignition key out of it – but, all of a sudden, he just drove off and kept it. He shouted something at me, but I couldn't hear what he said.'

'Oh,' said Judy. 'Could I have another sip of brandy, d'you think?' There could be no doubt about it now. James must have taken out the lamp and was taking it away to lose it.

Meanwhile James arrived home in an equally anxious state. It was quite plain that Judy had taken out the lamp. What was he to do with it? Throw it away or replace it later somewhere in the hotel? That seemed the better solution. Meantime, where should he keep it? It mustn't stay in Judy's bag. He took it out and put it in his pocket before he let himself into the house. But he realised the bulge would show in his pocket. He must get rid of it temporarily. As soon as he got into the house, he put it in a drawer in the hall. Then the nurse came in.

'Your father wants you, I believe,' she said. 'He's in the drawing room with your sister's fiancé.'

'Thanks awfully. I'll go straight to them. Sorry to appear in such a rush. But I gathered it was rather urgent.'

He went straight to the drawing room, where the judge was with Bernard Kent.

'Now, look, Jimmy,' said the judge, 'we've got to act quickly. I've told Bernard everything, and there's only one thing to do. It's obvious that York's not safe at large, and we'll have to prosecute. Warning him was no good. No – don't interrupt. I know the probable result – but there's no alternative. We're going to charge him with demanding money with menaces and arrest him at once. Bernard wants a statement of what he said to you.'

131

'There's no need,' said James.

'Really, Jimmy,' began Bernard.

'He's dead,' said James.

'What!' said the judge and Bernard together. 'How d'you know?' added the judge.

'He fell down the stairs at the Bull and broke his neck. I've just left him. He's dead, all right. You won't be troubled by him any more.'

'But how did it happen?'

'He was very drunk and must have fallen.'

'But why was he at the Bull anyway?'

'I sent for him.' said James. 'Judy and I decided to try and buy him off. We were going to get him to sign a sort of agreement. I'm sorry I didn't mention it to you, Father, but we knew you wouldn't be a party to paying the fellow anything. And, as things looked pretty desperate, we thought we'd try.'

'Jolly good thing, as it's turned out,' said Bernard. 'So long as no one's going to say you kicked him down the stairs.'

'I certainly didn't. He just fell.'

'All right, old boy. It was only a joke. In poor taste, I agree. Sorry.'

'That's all right,' said James. There was silence for a moment, and then he spoke again. 'Oh, my God,' he said.

It was a purely physical reaction. He had not meant to open his mouth, but it was the sudden realisation that he was talking to his sister's fiancé and that it was Bernard's duty to prove, if he could, that Judy had murdered the man, which made the ejaculation unavoidable.

'What's the matter?'

'Oh – nothing,' he said rather lamely. 'It's just the shock, the joy – if you like – that we've nothing more to worry about.'

'Does Judy know?'

'Yes. She got rather a shock naturally and she's just having a steadier. I said I'd go back and fetch her. But, as Bernard's here, perhaps he'd like to.'

James did not propose to leave the house without the lamp, if he could avoid it.

'Yes, of course. I'll go straight round.'

'Well,' said the judge, 'off you go. I think we'll all have a drink when you come back. I suppose one shouldn't feel cheerful at the death of a man – but I think this case is an exception. What a relief. Go and fetch Judy, and I'll open something special for the occasion.'

But to open something special of the kind which the judge had in mind, a corkscrew was necessary. And, of course, it would happen that, when James returned from the cellar with the bottle which his father had asked him to get, he found him looking for a corkscrew in the drawer where he had put the lamp.

'It's time we had a clear out,' said the judge. 'Look, here's some string, a lamp bulb, and – what's this – a hair net or something – oh – no – a tennis ball thing – ah – and here's a corkscrew. I suppose this is a dud. If so, why keep it? If not, let's put it somewhere we can find it when we want it. What is it? A forty? But that's funny, it's low voltage. Bit of luck I looked before we tried it. I suppose someone got it by mistake. Pity to waste it if it's any use to someone. I know. Take it down to the Bull and see if it's any use to them. They're not on the mains yet. Old Cumberland's got a bee in his bonnet about changing over.'

'All right, Father. I'll pop down in the morning.'

'Very well. I'll put it back here for the moment. But I don't expect to see it there again.'

'I won't forget,' said James.

CHAPTER THIRTEEN

Mr Bean Has an Idea

On the following morning, Alexander Bean was reading his paper at breakfast, when he saw something which made him stop his breakfast and go straight to the telephone. The something was a few lines in the 'Stop Press' of the Clarion which mentioned that a man called Sidney York had been killed by an accidental fall at the Bull Inn, Murrell Keeping. Such news travels fast. Mr Cumberland had called the local constable, the local constable had telephoned the nearest police station, and the information had been given out to the local press. Violent death is nearly always news, even on the highway. True, it has become so common there that one would hardly expect it to excite much attention. But deaths on the highway are frequently reported in the London press, though the reporting does not keep pace with the slaughter. Other violent deaths, even though obviously accidental, are almost always news. Whoever you are – fall out of a window, get burned to death, or even fall down the stairs and die, and you are almost sure of a place in the newspapers if that's what you want.

'Get me Robinson,' said Mr Bean, and, when Robinson had been got, he went on: 'Look, this is important. Give me three of your best men, put them in a fast car and send them round here. We're going off to Murrell Keeping. I think there's a story there. Keep a place for me on tomorrow's front page. Don't fill it up till you've got to. I may want to use the headline too. But you can change that at the last moment. We leave in half an hour. Let them bring some gear for the night. They may be staying. Yes – I said half an hour. We've no time to lose.'

While Mr Bean and his three reporters were on their way to Murrell Keeping, Colonel Brain was trimming one of the hedges in the Beverleys' garden. Soon after breakfast, the judge and Bernard, who had stayed the night, went for a stroll in the garden and met him. It was a Saturday and Bernard did not propose to go into Scotland Yard unless he was particularly wanted.

"Morning, Colonel,' said the judge. 'I don't think you've met my prospective son-in-law, Bernard Kent. He's an Assistant Commissioner at Scotland Yard.'

"Morning, judge. How d'you do, sir,' said the colonel. 'We shall have to be careful while you're around. There's no law against hedge-trimming on Saturday mornings yet, is there by any chance? It's so difficult to keep up with the regulations.'

'No, I think you're quite safe for the moment.'

'Good,' said the colonel. 'Well – we mustn't let any pigs have accidents until you're safely out of the way. Talking of which, that was a nasty thing at the Bull wasn't it? Poor devil. I saw him.'

'Very unfortunate,' said Bernard.

The judge said nothing.

'What's so extraordinary about it is the coincidence.'

'Coincidence?'

'Yes – most extraordinary. I'd only just had that trouble with the ginger-haired lunatic and, 'pon my word, someone does go and fall down the stairs.'

135

'Yes, it is strange,' said the judge.

'And what makes it so much stranger,' said the colonel, 'is that the light wasn't on.'

'I don't see why that makes it strange,' said Bernard. 'No doubt that's why it happened. I gather it's a death-trap. I shouldn't be surprised if the relatives made a claim on the Bull. From what I hear, it was asking for trouble. Surprised it's not happened before.'

'But that isn't it, my dear fellow, at all. Old Cumberland had put in an extra switch. And d'you know what happened? Someone had taken out the lamp.'

'What!' said the judge.

'I thought that'd surprise you,' went on the colonel. 'You judges don't like coincidences – sometimes don't believe in them, I suspect. I've heard you, my dear fellow – not you personally, I mean, but one of the others – what was his name – I forget – no – I know – Mr Justice Tring – I remember him saying, when the prisoner's defence depended on a large number of coincidences: "Are you really asking the jury to believe that by coincidence this happened" – I don't remember the exact facts – it was some time ago – "and, by coincidence, that happened, and, by coincidence, the other happened" and so forth and so on – you can hear him saying it, can't you, my dear fellow – "are you asking the jury to believe all that?" he said. "I hope they'll believe it," said the prisoner, not very happily, "because it happens to be true." "Oh, it happens to be true, does it," says his Lordship. "That will be for the jury to say." Then came the most extraordinary coincidence of all. The jury did believe it. At any rate, they said "Not guilty." Must have spoiled old Tring's lunch. He was dead set on a conviction. Had the black cap ready and the chaplain and all that. They even said "Not guilty" to manslaughter as well. You should have seen the old boy's face. He could have given him fifteen years for manslaughter. As a matter of fact, I was told afterwards by one of the counsel in the case that the chap had offered to plead guilty to manslaughter, but the judge wouldn't have it. "This is murder," he'd said. But the jury said it was not. When he'd recovered, old Tring said: "You're discharged. You're very lucky in your jury." Upon which, what d'you think the prisoner said? I'll give him full marks for it, I must say. "You've no right whatever to say that, my Lord," he said. And, 'pon my word, I thought old Tring would burst. You could see him thinking, "Can I send him to gaol for contempt?" And then I suppose he realised that probably the chap was right. Anyway, all he said was: "Behave yourself." You fellows always seem to fall back on that when you can't think of anything better. I must say it's quite effective in the normal way – but, on this occasion, it fell rather flat. Sorry – I seem to be talking a lot – and it's early in the morning for that.'

'Did you say the lamp was missing?' asked the judge.

'Yes, my dear fellow. Yes, and there was another thing too. Even more astonishing. I'd got so tied up with old Tring I almost forgot to tell you. This one'll shake you. At least, I hope it will. D'you know what I said to James and Judy two nights before it happened? When I came round after the lunatic had flung me out of the Bull?'

'No – what?'

'I'll tell you, my dear fellow – I'll tell you. And, if I may say so – it ought to stop you laughing at coincidences in the future. It's the most astonishing thing, I assure you. Are you really asking the jury to believe this – are you really?'

But the judge could not wait any longer. 'What was it you said, Colonel?' he interrupted.

'Just this, my dear fellow. You know what the row with the lunatic was about. You know what he was complaining to the Cumberlands about when I interrupted.'

'Yes – yes,' said the judge impatiently, 'but what did you say to James and Judy?'

'I'm coming to it, my dear fellow. Don't be so impatient. I couldn't talk to you like this in Court. That's what my young rascal of a nephew used to say to me when I was in the Army. He was in my battalion. I was a half-colonel and he was only a subaltern. And when he came to stay he used to call me all the names under the sun, said he'd like to do it when he was on parade but didn't want to be court martialled. Now, where had I got to?'

'You were going to tell us what you said to James and Judy.'

'Of course – I take as long to get to the point as some of your counsel do, I believe. Sometimes they don't get there at all – or sometimes there isn't a point to get to. I often wonder how you stand it. Listening to them drivelling all day. Still, it's what they're paid to do, I imagine. And, then, from time to time you must remember that you did it yourself once. That must make a difference, I suppose.'

'Yes,' said the judge, controlling himself.

'Well – I suppose you'd like me to get on with my work instead of gossiping to you. Still, it's not my fault if my employer stops me working, is it now? It was time for a breather, as a matter of fact. Oh, but I was going to tell you what I said to James and Judy. If it won't bore you, that is.'

'I should like to hear,' said the judge quietly.

'It really is amazing. Two days before this fellow kills himself because there isn't a lamp in the socket, I said to them: "If I wanted to kill a man, I'd ask him down for the night and take the bulb out." Now, what d'you think of that, my dear fellow? There's a coincidence for you.'

Neither the judge nor Bernard could say a word. Bernard did not know about the lamp, but he knew quite enough to be disturbed, but for the judge it was an almost paralysing blow.

'It's lucky the fellow was a friend. If they'd wanted him out of the way, it would have looked very funny, wouldn't it? Not that even then anyone would have believed it of either of them. But it just shows you, doesn't it, how dangerous it is to disbelieve in coincidences.'

The judge managed to say: 'Well – thank you, Colonel. Be seeing you later,' and he and Bernard walked away.

They said nothing at first. The judge could not make up his mind whether to mention the lamp. Then Bernard said: 'But it's preposterous. Neither of them would do it.' The judge said nothing. 'You don't think they did, do you?' Bernard went on. 'I know, of course, that there was motive and so on, but I'm sure they wouldn't have done such a thing. It must be terribly worrying for you, judge. I'm most awfully sorry. What are we going to do?'

'I've no idea,' said the judge. 'I shall have to tell you this. It may be worse than you think.'

'What d'you mean?'

'Last night I found a low-voltage bulb in a drawer in the hall. It's no use to us but the Bull could use it.'

'You're not suggesting – ?'

'I'm not suggesting anything – but it's a very unfortunate coincidence if the Bull is short of a lamp and we have one that we've never had any use for. We'd better speak to Jimmy at once and clear it up one way or the other.'

'It'll hardly be clearing it up – if it's the other.'

'I suppose you're right. Well – what's my duty? I'm a judge – and it's my son and daughter.'

'And what's mine? I'm an Assistant Commissioner and she's to be my wife.'

'I wish to heaven I'd had the fellow arrested at once. But it's no good thinking of that.'

And all this was happening just because three years previously Gilbert Swanley had walked into the offices of the *London Clarion* and applied for a job.

CHAPTER FOURTEEN

Mr Bean Makes Some Enquiries

A good many things were now happening at the same time. The law had been set in motion and the Coroner's officer was making the usual enquiries for the Coroner and a post-mortem was arranged. Mr Justice Beverley and Bernard Kent were considering their respective problems. James and Judy were waiting for something to happen. Neither discussed the matter with the other, each believing in the other's guilt and being determined to prevent that guilt being found out if humanly possible. It has been seen that the judge himself at the age of twenty-one – no doubt in extenuating circumstances but nevertheless quite deliberately – had committed perjury to help a brother officer. James and Judy were perfectly prepared to do the same, if necessary, to help each other. And Mr Bean and his three reporters had now arrived at the Bull. Mr Bean soon found Mr Cumberland.

'We're not open yet, I'm afraid,' he said.

'Good morning,' said Mr Bean affably. 'We don't want a drink, as a matter of fact – but I wondered if you had a room for the night.'

'Well,' said Mr Cumberland, 'we only have one room – and – ' he paused.

'Well – that's all right – one will do. I suppose you don't mind if two of these gentlemen use it.'

'No,' said Mr Cumberland. 'There are two beds but –'

'I suppose it's about the accident,' put in Mr Bean helpfully. 'The poor chap who was killed had it and you wondered if we'd mind.'

'D'you know about it already then?'

'Oh, yes. Bad news, I'm afraid, travels fast.'

'Well – that was it, as a matter of fact. I thought possibly – '

'That's quite all right. They won't mind in the least. Might we see it, d'you think?'

'Yes – certainly – but I must warn you about the stairs.'

'Stairs?'

'Yes – the stairs down which the unfortunate man fell.'

'Oh – he fell down the stairs, did he? I didn't know that. Are they unsafe then?'

'The stairs are all right, but if the light's not on at night and you don't know your way about, you can fall down them.'

'And that's what happened?'

'Yes.'

'Mr Justice Beverley lives in the neighbourhood, doesn't he?'

'Yes – he does, as a matter of fact.'

'He wasn't here at the time, by any chance?'

'No – but it's curious you should ask that.'

'Why?'

'Oh – because his son and daughter happened to be here.'

'Did they indeed? Just having a drink, I suppose?'

'Well – as a matter of fact they knew the chap who was killed. Not very well, I gather.'

'Really. It must have been a nasty shock for them.'

'It was. Miss Beverley fainted.'

'Did she really? Poor girl. I hope she's all right again.'

'Oh – yes – it was just the shock, you know.'

'Very natural.'

They went in to see the room and Mr Bean looked at the light by the dangerous staircase. 'I wonder why it wasn't on,' he said.

'There was a good reason for that,' said Mr Cumberland. 'There was no lamp in it.'

'I see,' said Mr Bean. 'Well – I suppose you can't be everywhere at the same time. Mistakes will happen. Accidents will happen.'

'Well, there certainly was an accident, but for the life of me I can't think how it happened. I'm not sure that I ought to mention all this, but I suppose it doesn't matter as it will all come out at the inquest. It's not as if there'd been foul play or anything.'

'Of course not,' said Mr Bean. 'Quite impossible. The inquest will be a mere formality. Cause of death – broken neck. Cause of broken neck – falling down the stairs. Cause of falling down the stairs – no light. Cause of no light – didn't know where the switch was, I suppose.'

'He may not have known that, it's true,' said Mr Cumberland, 'but if he had switched it on, it wouldn't have helped. I told you – there was no lamp in it.'

'Of course. Silly of me. I forgot. Are you worrying about their being down on you for forgetting?'

'I should be if I had forgotten – particularly in view of what happened a day or two ago.'

'I don't understand,' said Mr Bean. 'D'you mean you had put a lamp in?'

'I do. I put it in myself.'

'You don't mean to say it just went? It couldn't fall out.'

'Well – it could if I hadn't put it in properly. But I had. I'd tried it.'

'But you've got it in now. Where did you find it?'

'That's another one – we never did find it.'

'D'you mean to say the lamp has disappeared?'

'That's exactly what I do mean. That's the extraordinary thing. It's just disappeared.'

'I agree – that is strange. But what were you saying about something happening a day or two before?'

'Well, an escaped lunatic nearly fell down the stairs and he made a commotion about it and flung out one of our customers who remonstrated with him.'

'I see. Did everyone know about the row?'

'Well – not everyone, I suppose. But a Colonel Brain was the customer who was thrown out, and he's pretty well known round here.'

'Where does he live, might I ask?'

'Oakside Cottage – just down the road.'

'Well – it's been most kind of you to show us the room. D'you think we could have it for a week or so? I rather fancy we shall be down here for a bit.'

'You're not from the press by any chance?'

'Well, as a matter of fact, we are. My name is Bean. Alexander Bean. I don't suppose you've ever heard of me. I own the *London Clarion*.'

'We take the *Pemberton Gazette* here.'

'Pemberton's the nearest town, I suppose.'

'That's right. I hope you're not going to print anything that I've said. Not that I've said anything I shouldn't, but, you know, one just has a feeling about getting into the papers. Some people like it, I know, bathing girls and such like, but we don't care for it much here.'

'My dear Mr – Mr – '

'Cumberland.'

'My dear Mr Cumberland, you need have no fear on that score. My newspapers are the soul of discretion. This interview won't be mentioned.'

'That's very good of you.'

'Not at all – you ought to take the *Clarion*, you know. I'm sure you'll find a lot of your neighbours do.'

'I don't get much time for reading the papers.'

'Quite so. Well – I think two of you'd better stay here. George and Martin? Right. And I'll take Cyril into Pemberton. But, first of all, let's take a stroll. Good morning, Mr Cumberland. I dare say we shall be meeting again. Thank you so much for everything.'

Half an hour later a car pulled into the drive of the Beverleys' house and George got out. He did not look in the least like the reporter he was. His looks and his manner were more those of a middle-aged doctor. He was accordingly extremely valuable for getting information from places where the ordinary reporter was barred. He rang the bell. Judy opened the door.

'I'm most awfully sorry,' began George, 'but I wonder if I could beg a favour.'

'Yes?' said Judy enquiringly.

'I've a most important telephone call to make and the box here is out of order. If I don't get through at once, it'll be too late. I know I shouldn't trouble you – but could you possibly allow me?'

'Oh – very well – certainly,' said Judy. 'It's just here in the hall. Is it a long-distance call?'

'It is, as a matter of fact – but, of course – you'll let me pay, please. I'll find out what the charge is. Thank you very much. It is most kind.' He went to the telephone and asked for a personal call to a Mr Alan Jones in a large hotel in Wales. He was told, as he expected, to hang up the receiver and wait.

'I do hope they'll be able to get it quickly. Do they usually keep one waiting long?' he asked anxiously.

'Naturally it depends on the time of day and the place. It shouldn't be too bad now.'

'Thank you. I hope I'm lucky.' There was a pause.

'A charming village this is. I've not been here before.'

'It is nice, isn't it.'

'I tried to telephone from the Bull – but there was a queue for the 'phone there. I was surprised. I suppose it's either betting, or market day somewhere in the neighbourhood.'

Judy said nothing.

'Is there normally such a crowd there?'

'Is there a crowd at the Bull?' she asked.

'Well – any number's a crowd if they're all waiting to use the telephone and so are you. About half a dozen chaps or so. Seems to have been an accident of some kind there from what they were saying.'

'Yes – there was.'

'I'm so sorry. No one hurt badly, I hope.'

'A man was killed.'

'How dreadful. No one you knew, I trust.'

'He was a stranger here.'

'You don't expect accidents in a place like this. May I ask what it was?'

'I'd rather not talk about it, if you don't mind. I was at the Bull at the time. A man fell down some back stairs and was killed.'

'How very distressing for you. I'm so very sorry. I wouldn't have mentioned the subject, if I'd known. I do apologise. What a time they're taking over that call. It'll be too late in a moment.' Then, under his breath, he said: 'Poor devil.'

'There'll be an inquest, I suppose?'

'I suppose so.'

'If you were there, you may have to give evidence. How horrible for you. That must be worrying you a lot.'

He waited for a moment and then said: 'D'you know – does Archie Preston happen to be the Coroner for these parts? I know he's somewhere round here.'

'He is, as a matter of fact.'

'I know him very well. Look – you've been so very kind to me this morning. I wonder if I could help you. Nothing improper, of course. But Archie knows me well, and if I could assure him that there was nothing you could say to help, you mightn't have to give evidence.'

'It's very kind of you – but – ' and Judy paused.

'Has the Coroner's officer been to take a statement from you yet?'

'No.'

'Well – he will – of course. Purely routine matter, you know. But the Coroner will want a statement from everyone who was on the premises at the time. Of course, if the Coroner had your statement already, he wouldn't have to send his officer to you. I do hope you don't think I'm interfering. But, if you'll forgive me, you looked so unhappy, I should like to be of help.'

'I don't think so, thank you,' said Judy. 'I shall attend the inquest if I'm wanted. It's just rather upsetting, that's all.'

'Of course it is. That call is taking a long time.'

There was silence for a moment or two and then, quite quietly but looking at her intently, George said: 'What d'you know about the missing lamp?'

Judy was quite unable to control the fright the question gave her, and realising the guilty appearance she must have given, she relied upon anger. 'I know nothing about any lamp,' she said angrily. 'And who are you anyway? I think you'd better cancel that call and go. I'll cancel it for you. Now, kindly go.'

'Really,' said George, 'what a fuss to make over a simple question. But I'll remember the answer. You know nothing of any missing lamp, but it makes you very angry – and perhaps a little frightened – to be asked about it.'

'Get out,' said Judy.

'Of course,' said George. As he started to go the telephone rang.

'I'll answer it,' said Judy. 'Kindly go.'

'Certainly,' said George. 'It doesn't really matter now.'

Judy answered the telephone. The operator informed her that no Alan Jones could be found at the hotel in question and then proceeded to discuss the accident to Mr York for as long as Judy would allow her.

As soon as she'd finished she rushed to find Bernard and threw herself sobbing into his arms.

'Oh – darling, I'm so frightened,' she said.

'What is it, darling?'

'There was a horrible man who pretended he wanted to use the telephone and then he suddenly asked me – ' and she broke down.

'What did he ask you?' he said gently.

'No – I can't tell you – but be kind to me, please be kind to me.'

This was quite as bad for Bernard as it could be. He was desperately fond of Judy. That came first. But he had a strong regard for duty. He wanted to help Judy – he wanted to do what was right. By asking questions he might put both of them in a worse position. He put his arms round her and kissed her instead.

'I am with you always,' he said. He was about to add 'whatever happens,' but checked himself in time. People who are afraid that something is going to happen do not like to be reminded that it may very well happen.

Meanwhile, the judge had decided that he must speak to James. The matter was far too serious to be left uncertain.

'Jimmy,' he said, 'I'm sorry to have to worry you, but I must ask you some questions. That lamp – d'you know where it came from?'

'Well – as a matter of fact, I do.'

'Where then?'

'From the Bull.'

'Why did you do it, Jimmy?'

'Do what?'

'Take it out?'

'I didn't – nor did Judy.'

'Who did then?'

'I've no idea. Judy wasn't there anyway when it happened.'

'Where was she?'

'She was in the bar. I was in the lounge talking to York. He went upstairs.'

'Was the light on?'

'It couldn't have been.'

'Where was the lamp then?'

'I don't know.'

'But you brought it home.'

'I meant I didn't know where it was when he fell. I found it later.'

'But where? And why did you bring it home?'

James did not answer.

'And why didn't you say all this when I saw it last night?'

'It does sound pretty thin, I admit,' said James.

149

'It's not just thin,' said the judge. 'No one would believe it for a moment. People don't come away from hotels with electric light bulbs in their pockets.'

'It wasn't in my pocket.'

'Where was it then?'

James paused. Then – 'It was in my hand when I got into the car and I put it on the seat.'

'But why did you bring it home?'

'I can't think. I wish I hadn't.'

'And why didn't you tell me last night?'

James didn't answer. Finally he smiled slightly and said: 'I'm not a terribly good liar, I'm afraid. But please don't ask any more at the moment. I'll try to improve on it later. You won't have to give evidence of this conversation, I hope.'

'Heaven knows who'll have to give evidence about what.'

'If it was a letter, you could burn it. If it's a conversation, you can forget it.'

'Look, Jimmy,' said the judge, 'you know I only want to help – just as you did. But I can't if you don't tell me the truth.'

'Can you – if I do?'

CHAPTER FIFTEEN

The Enquiries Continue

By the time George had left Judy, Cyril had found Colonel Brain. He was clipping a hedge.

'Good afternoon,' he said. 'Thirsty work?'

'I'm glad to say it is,' said the colonel.

'I don't follow that argument,' said Cyril. 'You might just as well say it's nice to have an itch in order that you can scratch it.'

'Well, it is, now I come to think of it,' said Colonel Brain.

'Isn't it nicer not to have an itch at all?'

'I can't say that I've studied the problem very closely,' said the colonel, 'but now that you mention it, I can think of several analogies which would support my case. For example – it's nice to be hungry if you know there's a good dinner to come.'

'I expect you're right, and, talking of dinner, do they give you a good meal at the Bull?'

'Well – they're a bit at sixes and sevens at the moment, but normally they're pretty good.'

'You're referring to the accident, I suppose?'

'I am.'

'Is the inquest fixed yet?'

'I don't know.'

'Rotten bad luck it was for everyone. D'you know anything about the chap?'

'Not a thing, my dear fellow. Am I being pumped, by the way? Just like to know, you know. It won't make any difference. You can't pump water out of a dry well.'

'Come and have one then.'

'I didn't mean that, my dear fellow. And anyway if you're a reporter, as I strongly suspect, you wouldn't approve of my drinking. Ginger pop's my line.'

'You don't say?'

'I do. Horrible, isn't it?'

'Then why do it?'

'I like it, my dear fellow. Can't stick the other stuff. But you'd think it horrible to knock back ginger pop, wouldn't you?'

'I can take it with gin, you know.'

'Yes, my dear fellow, looking at you I should imagine you could. But no, I wasn't cadging for a drink. I just meant I didn't know anything. No use to you, my dear fellow – no use at all. And anyway the only thing that would interest you would be the coincidence.'

'What coincidence?'

'Can't be done, my dear fellow. Sealed lips and all that.'

'But why on earth? It sounds a good story.'

'It is a good story, my dear fellow, but you must wait for the inquest. Contempt of court to tell you before.'

'Contempt, my foot. It's a free country.'

'So you say, my dear fellow, but there's still such a thing as contempt of court. I nearly got put away once – by the Lord Chief Justice – but that's another story. But we soldiers aren't as dumb as you think. Never talk to the press until the case is over. Otherwise you'll be for it and all that.'

'That doesn't apply to a Coroner's inquest.'

'So you say, my dear fellow, but I don't take any risks. Near as a touch he sent me to prison.'

'Who?'

'I was just about to tell you, my dear fellow – only you wouldn't ask. The Lord Chief Justice. I've been there, you see. He was quite friendly after a time, but at first I thought I was for it. Broad arrows and all that, except that they don't wear them any more. Now would you say you've got anything out of me, my dear chap?'

'Not a thing – except that there was a coincidence.'

'And that reminds me – another coincidence. It's time for me to knock off. D'you think I'm worth a ginger pop at the Bull, my dear fellow? Tell me candidly, d'you think I'm worth it?'

'Well, candidly, I doubt it, but I'll have a try.'

'The trouble is you can't get a chap to talk on ginger pop. Wherever it goes, it doesn't go to the head.'

'True enough.'

'Of course, I talk a good deal without anything and I don't mind telling you, my dear chap, I enjoy it.'

'That's what I want you to do – talk and enjoy yourself.'

'So I shall – but not to the press before an inquest. It was my housekeeper that warned me, as a matter of fact. "There'll be some of those reporter chaps about," she said. "Keep your wits about you or they'll open you up like a sardine tin." I thought that was rather good – like a sardine tin. How d'you think she thought of that, my dear fellow? Never thought she had any imagination before. But she must have. "Like a sardine tin," she said. And that's another coincidence.'

'Oh,' said Cyril, a little more interested.

'I had them for breakfast. P'raps that's how she thought of it.'

Although little was to be obtained from Colonel Brain, Mr Bean and his team had done very well. He left them in the country and went back to London. On the following day he went to see Mr Rounce.

'I don't know if you've read about that accident at Murrell Keeping,' he began.

'I can't say that I have,' said Mr Rounce.

'No, I didn't expect you would have. But you will. I want you to instruct counsel to appear at the inquest. I should have told you that a man fell down the back stairs at an inn and was killed.'

'Who is counsel to represent?'

'Silly of me. I hadn't thought of that. The next-of-kin, I suppose.'

'Did you know the man then?'

'I met him once, but I want to see his next-of-kin are protected. They may have a good claim against the inn proprietor for negligence or something.'

'Well – that's easily arranged, Mr Bean, but I should just like to have a retainer from the next-of-kin, whoever he or she is.'

'You shall have it. I'll send it in the morning.'

'Who would you like me to instruct? It's not, of course, a case for Gillingham, although he would, no doubt, go to an inquest for you. But he'd want a large fee.'

'No – I don't want Gillingham for this. As a matter of fact, that's why I've come to see you.'

'Oh?'

'Yes – about the choice of counsel. I don't want an ordinary chap.'

'I don't follow,' said Mr Rounce.

'Well – strange things may happen – important people may get involved. Important people in the law, I mean – to be more precise, a High Court judge may get involved.'

'I see.'

'I want someone who won't be frightened to speak up. No trade union rules or honour among thieves stuff. I want someone who won't worry if he gets into trouble himself.'

'I beg your pardon.'

Mr Bean repeated his statement. 'You see,' he added, 'I may want to do things some people wouldn't like to do – particularly if a judge were involved. A Coroner's Court's a funny court. You can do anything if you can shout louder than the Coroner. And he can do anything if he can shout louder than you. And what's shouted finds its way into the newspapers. Now, I'm not going to tell you any more for the moment, but, of course, I'll give you the material to brief him in time for the inquest. Or, better still, I'll brief him myself in conference. Now, there's an odd chap called Frith Wyndham. I've heard him shouting nonsense at the Old Bailey. He's just what I want for this case. I'll tell him what to ask and he's just the chap to shout the Coroner down. He may be turned out in the end. Or he may turn the Coroner out. I don't mind. I want a man who'll make a blazing row, whatever happens. You see there may be nothing in it, but I've got quite a lot of material to suggest – only to suggest, mind you, that that accident was not as accidental as all that. The Coroner will try to keep that sort of thing out. If there's anything in it, that won't matter very much, as I'll force the police to do something about it. But if it won't stand up, I want someone who'll make the most news of it. Mud sticks, Mr Rounce.'

'So I have observed,' said Mr Rounce with dignity. 'But it is not going to stick to my firm. I'm afraid, Mr Bean, that I must ask you to take this particular piece of business elsewhere, and if in consequence you wish to remove all your work, I shall quite understand it and will do everything to assist any solicitors you may appoint as our successors.'

'Dear me. What a fuss,' said Mr Bean affably. Lunatics like Mr Bean sometimes take offence when they are least expected to and vice versa.

'Of course, I'll take this elsewhere. You've always told me you don't care for criminal work. But please carry on with the rest of my work, unless you're tired of it.'

'Very well,' said Mr Rounce. 'Just as you wish.'

'Could you by any chance recommend some other solicitors who would take on this job?'

'I don't want to be rude, Mr Bean, but I certainly could not recommend any solicitors who would.'

'Well – that's a pretty turn of phrase, Mr Rounce, if I may say so, and, upon that note, I'll go and find someone for myself.'

It was not long before Mr Bean had found Mr Tewkesbury of Bogg, Tewkesbury & Co. He reeked of whisky and was exactly what Mr Bean wanted.

'Your reputation is growing, you see, Mr Tewkesbury.'

'Oh, that,' said Mr Tewkesbury. 'Oh – that was just unfortunate, sir. These policemen – they think anyone whose breath smells of alcohol is drunk.'

'I wasn't referring to what I take it is a report of some case in which you were personally concerned,' said Mr Bean.

'Oh – ' said Mr Tewkesbury. 'It was nothing. I was said to have been drunk in charge of a bicycle. There's a ridiculous charge, sir, if you like. A bicycle. I ask you, sir. As a matter of fact, the bicycle was really in charge of me. I haven't ridden one for many years and – '

'Yes, yes,' said Mr Bean, who had not come to listen to Mr Tewkesbury's reminiscences. He told Mr Tewkesbury what he required, he offered him a handsome fee, he paid him £25 on account, and everything was arranged to the complete satisfaction of both parties. Later the greatest satisfaction was given to a third party, Mr Frith Wyndham, when he received his first and only brief marked fifty guineas. It was described as: 'Brief to counsel to represent the next-of-kin,' but it should have been called 'Brief to counsel to make the hell of a row.' It is not recorded that any brief so marked has ever been delivered to counsel, but, undoubtedly, the more polite language has sometimes served to cover that real purpose.

Having arranged the briefing of counsel on behalf of the next-of-kin (Mr Tewkesbury did not worry about such trifling matters as retainers or the existence of his client so long as he was paid by someone), Mr Bean went to find the next-of-kin. He already had Sidney's address and he called there. He was advised by someone on the ground floor to try the second floor. He tried it. The door was opened by Martha.

'Are you Mrs York by any chance?' asked Mr Bean.

Martha hesitated. Then: 'In a sort of way, I suppose I am.'

'I'm afraid I have some very bad news for you.'

'D'you mean about him?'

'About your – your husband – yes.'

'I read about that. He's dead, isn't he?'

'I'm afraid so.'

'I shan't have to pay for the funeral, will I – seeing that we weren't actually married. I've only been with him six months, as a matter of fact.'

'Oh – no – Mrs – Mrs – York. That will all be arranged if you'll be good enough to sign this paper.'

'I don't like signing things.'

'This is to your advantage, in fact. It's only an authority to solicitors to represent you at the inquest. You don't know of any relatives he had, I suppose?'

'He never mentioned any.'

'Good. Now, you just sign this and you'll have no more to worry about.'

'It's quite all right, is it? I once signed an agreement for my husband – my real one, I mean, and I had a terrible time over that. It was a washing-machine. He tried to put me in it. Fancy going round and round like they do. I should have been dizzy. But I was too big to go in, you see. So he just bashed me instead. Haven't liked signing things since then.'

'I quite understand,' said Mr Bean, 'but I assure you that this will be quite all right.'

'That's what the other fellow said. My husband ought to have put him in the washing-machine. He wouldn't have come out so smooth as he talked to me.'

'Ah – this is quite different. You'll have no need to worry about this.'

'That's what the man with the television said, but I got bashed just the same and they took the television away.'

'I assure you this is nothing to do with a washing-machine, a television set or a vacuum cleaner.'

'I didn't say anything about a vacuum cleaner. How did you know I had one? And suppose the price was a bit low – how should I know where he got it from? That doesn't mean to say I knew it was stolen, does it? Are you from the police?'

'My dear Mrs York, I assure you I'm not from the police. Now all this document says – is – there – I'll read it to you. "I hereby authorise Messrs Bogg, Tewkesbury & Co to instruct counsel to appear on my behalf at the inquest on Sidney York." That's all. Now that can't hurt you. And you'll have nothing to pay. Indeed, I thought this might be of some help to you in your sorrow.'

And Mr Bean produced a five-pound note.

'Oh, thank you – you are kind.'

'Now if you just sign here. What's your Christian name?'

'Martha.'

'Very well then. Just sign here – Martha York. That's right. Now you'll have nothing to worry about at all. We just want to see that your – your – Mr York and you get justice.'

Martha gave a slight smile. It was her first for a long time. 'I expect he's getting it now,' she said.

'I'm sure I hope so,' said Mr Bean. 'He's now before his Maker.'

'When my time comes,' said Martha, 'I'd like to ask his Maker something.'

'Oh?' said Mr Bean, a little surprised at Martha's gathering initiative.

'Yes – I'd like to ask Him why He made him like that.'

'Well,' said Mr Bean, 'I'm glad you're bearing up so well. It must have been a great shock for you. You'll read all about the inquest in the *London Clarion*.'

'Will I be in the papers?'

'I'm not sure that you will, but he will.'

'Oh, him. It wouldn't be the first time. He kept some of the bits about himself. Used to add 'em up when he had nothing better to do.'

Mr Bean took his leave of Martha, and went to his office. He sent for the Editor.

'Start building up this case, will you, Frank? Nothing definite, you know, but this kind of thing. "Had the dead man a secret? It is believed that there will be strange revelations at the inquest on Sidney York, etc etc." You know the sort of idea. Keep it on the front page. The inquest's on Tuesday. So build it up fairly quickly so that you can use it as the main headline if we want to, unless the Iron Curtain's been raised or something we must put first. Yes, it's all going very nicely, thank you.'

Some days before the inquest the Coroner's officer, PC Swanage, called to take statements from James and Judy.

'Very sorry to trouble you,' he said, 'but, as you seem to have been the last people to see the deceased alive, the Coroner would just like a short statement. Only a formality, you know. Then he'll decide whether he wants you at the inquest.'

'Oh – that's quite all right,' said James. 'My sister and I quite understand. Shall I write it out or will you take it down?'

'Well – if it's not too long, sir, I'll take it down.'

'Oh – it's quite short. My sister and I were having a drink at the Bull. The dead man happened to be staying there. I'd met him once before and I had a chat with him in the lounge. My sister came in for a short time and then went either to the lavatory on the ground floor or the bar, I forget which. Mr York went up to his room. Then Colonel Brain came in and, just after him, Mr Cumberland, and, while we were having a chat, there was a crash. We rushed out and found he'd fallen down the back stairs. And that's really all.'

'Did you notice if the light was on upstairs?'

'I didn't until after the crash, when the colonel or Mr Cumberland pointed out that it wasn't. Apparently, from what I've heard since, the bulb wasn't in.'

'Well – thank you very much, sir. You don't, of course, know anything about why the bulb wasn't in?'

'No, I'm afraid not.'

'Well – I didn't expect you would, sir. And now, Miss Beverley, can you remember where you were when the crash came?'

'I was just coming out of the lavatory on the ground floor. I'd been to the bar just before that.'

'I see. Thank you very much, miss. Of course you don't know anything about the missing lamp either, I suppose?'

'Missing, did you say?'

'Yes, miss, apparently it's disappeared. But knowing the way they do things there, it wouldn't surprise me at all. He'll forget to wake up one of these days. If you ask me, there never was a lamp there at all and Mr Cumberland has just imagined it. But, there it is, I wouldn't say a word against him – only, if I could remember all he'd forgotten, I'd be a walking encyclopaedia. I lost £10 once over his forgetting to put a bet on for me. Oh – it was quite legal and all that. On the telephone, you know. But £10 is a lot of money. The missus fancied the horse, as a matter of fact. I've never heard the last of it. Well, thank you very much, miss – thank you, sir. I hope we shan't have to trouble you – but that's up to Mr Preston, of course.'

'Well, that seemed all right,' said Judy after the police officer had gone. 'Will they ask us any other questions if we have to go?'

'One can't tell, of course. But the great thing to remember is that you never went upstairs. No one saw you except me. So they can't prove you did.'

'But what about you?'

'No one saw me go up either and you're the only person who knew that I did.'

'Where's the lamp now?'

'Back at the Bull. There's a sort of junk cupboard they've got, just off the lounge. I popped it in there. So everything should be OK – as long as they don't ask father about it.'

'Why should that matter?'

'Well, he knows I brought the lamp home. He saw it. And I lied about it at first, too. But I don't think it matters. There's no reason why they should ask him anything about it. It would be awkward if they did though. However – cheer up, old girl. You see, Swanage didn't even ask to see father. They think he's nothing to do with it. And they're quite right. Ah – here's someone to brighten you up.'

It was Bernard, looking very serious.

'I'll clear out,' said James.

They said nothing at first, after James had gone. Then Bernard spoke.

'Judy, you must tell me something. You know I'll do anything in the world to help you – but I can't if I don't know the truth. Please tell me. You do trust me, don't you?'

'Of course – I trust you – but you're a policeman – is it good for you to know everything? Suppose I told you – I took the lamp out myself – that would put you in a horrible position, wouldn't it? I didn't, as a matter of fact, but, if you knew that I did, how could you help me and do your job at the same time?'

'I don't know. P'raps I shan't do my job. I don't know that either. But what I do know is that it's hopeless working in the dark. It's something to know that you didn't take the lamp out. That means, of course – ' he paused. 'Tell me – how did a low-voltage lamp get into that drawer?'

She did not answer.

'You must tell me. How did it?' He opened the drawer. 'Well – it isn't there now anyway. Your father told me one was there. What's happened to it?'

'It's no use, darling. I just can't tell you.'

'But you know, don't you? I can see that you know. I know you wouldn't lie to me. That means that James took it out. I'm not asking you to admit that. But tell me – and this is vital – did you know he was going to? Did you?'

'No.'

'Well – thank God for that. Nothing can happen to you.'

'I'm not worried about myself.'

'Maybe not – but I am.'

Meanwhile the judge was tackling James again. 'Jimmy, the inquest's on Tuesday. I must know where we are. For heaven's sake, tell me the truth. You'll never get away with a pack of lies, in any event. Do tell me what really happened. And then we can see where we are. I know I'm right. I always did that with my clients when I was at the Bar and I was right then. I'm right now. Tell me – I'll believe you – tell me – did you take the lamp out?'

'No.'

'Then it was Judy.'

'If it was her, are you any better off for knowing it?'

'I'm no worse off. Did you know she was going to take it out?'

'No.'

'Why did you bring it back here then?'

James hesitated. 'Oh – well – I suppose you're right. It was in her bag.'

'I see. But how did you come to have her bag if you didn't know anything about what was in it?'

'Colonel Brain brought it to me. I wanted the ignition key. He went to get it for me. Apparently she wasn't feeling too good at the time, so he brought the bag along.'

'Did he see the lamp in it?'

'No. But he must have thought I behaved queerly. I put my hand in to get the key and at once felt the lamp. It gave me such a shock – I just shouted something at him and drove off.'

'Then you really knew nothing about it till then?'

'I told you I didn't.'

'I'm sorry. D'you know if she got the idea suddenly?'

163

'I do, as a matter of fact. Colonel Brain suggested it.'

'Oh yes, he told me.'

'I wonder who else he's told,' said James. 'With all these reporters about the place. Oh – my God – I suppose he'll tell the Coroner's officer.'

'I'm afraid he may – and if he does – well, Archie Preston will be bound to have to ask you about it. I don't know what to do.'

'I thought you said that if you knew the truth it'd be a help. Suppose you were a barrister and advising a client. What would you do?'

'It depends on who I was advising. You're all right. But Judy – ' he broke off. 'I would advise her to refuse to give evidence,' he went on, after a moment. 'Indeed, if she admitted her guilt to me, I should certainly do so. But then you'd have to give evidence and you'd prove her guilt. If you'd been in it together, of course, you could refuse to give evidence too.'

'Well – we'll assume I was in it then.'

'It won't do, Jimmy, for a dozen different reasons. In any event it's an implicit confession by both of you if you refuse to give evidence. For people in your position, to refuse can only mean one thing. And it's all my fault, really.'

'Nonsense, father. It's no one's fault really, except York's. But, if you don't know what we can do, I certainly don't.'

If Gilbert Swanley had known what repercussions his application for the post of solicitor was going to have, he would certainly never have applied for it. Fortunately one does not know these things. Otherwise one would never do anything at all and even that might prove disastrous for someone.

Colonel Brain was in his most expansive mood when the Coroner's officer called on him.

CHAPTER SIXTEEN

Colonel Brain's Statement

'A statement, my dear fellow?' he said. 'Certainly. I've been waiting for this moment. They've been trying to pump me all the time, but I wouldn't have it. No – I said. I'm keeping this for the Coroner.'

'Thank you very much, sir. Now, would you tell me quite briefly what you know of the accident, sir?'

'Briefly?' said the colonel. 'Impossible. It's a long story. In fact, I'm not sure where to begin.'

PC Swanage repressed a sigh. He was very keen on his garden and this was the last statement he had to take that day. 'Mr Preston only wants the bare facts, you know, sir.'

'The bare facts, certainly,' said the colonel. 'But he wants all the facts, doesn't he? The facts, the whole facts and nothing but the facts. Take a chair, my dear fellow, and make yourself at home.'

This time, PC Swanage did give a small sigh, but the colonel did not notice and the constable sat down and resigned himself to the inevitable.

'Now, let me see,' said the colonel, 'I've never given evidence at an inquest before. Is the oath the same as at a court martial?'

'I'm afraid I've never given evidence at a court martial, sir.'

'No, of course. Well, never mind. There's a card, no doubt, to read it from. I suppose the Coroner will want my full particulars?'

'Just your name and address, sir.'

'But surely previous experience counts for something? Old Archie Preston knows me, of course, but he's got to pretend he doesn't. I've got to pretend I don't know him. That's justice. All fair and above board. Kissing doesn't go by favour. Everyone's equal in the eye of the law. See what I mean, Swanage?'

'Yes, sir,' said Swanage. 'Shall I write that down, sir?'

'Oh – no – thank you. These are just a few preliminary observations.'

As PC Swanage was obviously not going to be able to get to his garden, he decided to have a nap instead. 'Will you tell me when you get to the statement part, sir, and then I'll start writing? Will you say it rather loud, please, sir. Like this. Statement begins here.'

'Excellent, my dear fellow, excellent. Statement begins here. Most efficient. Reminds me of my orderly room. Statement begins here – I must remember that. No – I wasn't starting, my dear fellow. Just liked the expression. Statement begins here. No, not yet, my dear chap. I'll tell you when to begin – I'll say – now, I won't say it, but you know what I'm not saying, my dear chap; I'm just not saying it in case you start too soon, which you would do if I said: Statement begins here – no, not yet, my dear fellow – before I was ready to begin, if you follow what I mean. Now, where had I got to?'

PC Swanage was unable to assist the colonel. 'Ah – yes – a few preliminary observations. Now, the first thing I want to say is – don't take this down – ' PC Swanage had no intention of taking it down. Indeed, he was beginning to wonder if he could simply tell the Coroner that Colonel

Brain knew nothing about it. But then he reminded himself that Mr Cumberland would say the colonel was there. But it really was rather intolerable. He couldn't get to his garden and he couldn't in fact have a nap. He was finding the colonel horribly fascinating.

'In the first place, I think too much fuss is being made about this altogether. What do we want with the press and all that? Let the fellow fall down and break his neck in peace, I say. And these coincidences. I've been thinking them over in the last few days, and, if you ask me, they're just a red herring. Is the fellow dead? Yes. Why? Because he fell down the stairs. What more d'you want? All this talk about lamps and so on – what's it got to do with it? The man fell down the stairs, didn't he? What more d'you want? It's bad luck on the chap, mind you. I'm glad it wasn't me – but these things happen. It's no good saying they don't, because they do. It happened this time, didn't it? That proves it. So don't let me hear you say they don't happen, because they do. You or anyone else. I'm getting a bit tired of these people who say: "Don't worry, it may never happen." That's the spirit of the age. Not surprising things don't get done. They even have things printed in offices and so on. "Don't worry, it may never happen." What they ought to have – what we'd have had in my battalion if we'd needed anything – which we didn't – things were different in those days – what we'd have had would have been "Worry like hell. It's going to happen." Then you might get something done. That's my first point. I don't want any of this written down, you know, but my statement will read better if I work myself into it. One doesn't often have a chance like this.'

'You wouldn't like to tell me what you saw, sir?' put in PC Swanage, seeing that the colonel for the moment lacked inspiration.

'Saw?' said the colonel. 'Nothing, positively nothing.'

'Well, thank you very much, sir. I'll tell the Coroner,' said PC Swanage, and got up to leave.

'But don't you want to know what I heard, man?'

'Very well, sir, what did you hear?'

'A noise.'

'Like someone falling downstairs, sir?'

'Exactly – and what's more – it was someone falling downstairs.'

'Ah – but you didn't see him fall, did you, sir?'

'I saw him afterwards,' said the colonel. 'He was dead. I'm not frightened of dead men. Seen too many too often. I remember once – but this would probably make you sick. Funny how some things – nothing whatever to do with food – make people sick. I used to tell this story in the Club – it was true you know – I call it a story, but that doesn't mean it was made up – oh no, my dear chap – it was true as I'm standing here – well – I used to tell it at the Club and it was remarkable how the room thinned out. I'd come in – everyone delighted to see me – then I'd stand in front of the fire – winter or summer – just a habit, you know – and then I'd begin. "This is going to make you sick," I'd start, and, one by one, they'd troop out. I could see them getting greener and greener. Then the secretary came to me in the end. "Don't do it again, please, old man," he said. "Not after dinner, anyway." A trifle crude that, I thought – "Not after dinner." However, I think I can tell when to stop.'

'Well – in that case,' said PC Swanage, 'I think I'll be getting along. I'll tell the Coroner you heard a noise like someone falling downstairs, you went out and found a dead man. That right, sir?'

'You've left something out.'

'What, sir?'

'He had fallen down the stairs.'

'But you didn't see him, sir.'

'I know, but it was a plain deduction. Dammit, man, the body was at the bottom of the stairs. It wasn't at the top. He hadn't fallen up them. It wouldn't have made the same noise, falling up them, anyway.'

'Quite so, sir.'

'You speak as though I weren't allowed to put two and two together. A noise like someone falling downstairs, a body at the bottom of the stairs. What would anyone say? He'd fallen down the stairs, of course. It's obvious.'

'Very well, sir. Statement begins here. Colonel Brain says he heard a noise and that a man had fallen down the stairs and was dead. He saw the body.'

'Yes,' said the colonel, 'that's all right – as far as it goes – but you'd better add something.'

'Yes, sir?'

'That I didn't see him fall down the stairs. Don't want to mislead anybody, you know.'

CHAPTER SEVENTEEN

Counsel and Solicitor

On the following Tuesday, Mr Frith Wyndham and Mr Tewkesbury caught the nine o'clock train for Pemberton. Mr Wyndham was in very good form. He had a carnation in his buttonhole, a large number of different coloured pencils, three notebooks, *Stone's Justices' Manual*, and an old brief called *The King against Brown and Others*. He always carried it around with him, except at the Old Bailey and London Sessions, where it was known too well. It was marked 26 guineas (including a conference fee) and it was a very old brief indeed. But he brushed it up from time to time, except for the date, which he had expunged. He had never been paid the 26 guineas, but he thought it good for solicitors to see that they were briefing (on the rare occasions when they did brief him) a man who had been thought worth 26 guineas – marked on the brief anyway. He had not met Mr Tewkesbury before, but somehow or other they recognised each other on the platform and got onto the train together.

'I don't think,' began Mr Wyndham, 'I have had the pleasure of appearing for your firm before, Mr Tewkesbury.'

'No, sir,' said Mr Tewkesbury. 'Is there a buffet car on this train?'

'I'm afraid not.'

'Well – if you'll excuse me, sir. Fortunately I have made provision for such an emergency, sir.' He drank from a flask, and then went on: 'It isn't heart or nerves. It's because I like it, sir.'

'I see,' said Mr Wyndham. He was glad he had had half the fee in advance. Mr Tewkesbury had had the whole fee, but it was too much to expect that it would reach Mr Wyndham intact. Indeed, it was touch and go whether he got any of it, but Mr Bean, who considered that the labourer was worthy of his hire and who knew some of the ways of solicitors like Mr Tewkesbury, had asked to see counsel's receipt. So Mr Tewkesbury, much against his will, had been forced to pay over half the fee in order to get a receipt for the whole.

'Want it to show the client and haven't my cheque book on me. Send you the rest tomorrow.'

Mr Wyndham's clerk, without difficulty, persuaded Mr Wyndham to sign a receipt for the full amount. After all, the balance was coming in the morning, wasn't it? And Mr Tewkesbury had hinted that, unless he got a receipt for the whole, he wouldn't pay anything at all. Mr Bean did not know all the ways of solicitors like Mr Tewkesbury.

'This is a most interesting case,' said Mr Wyndham, after a pause. 'Might end up anywhere.'

'It's being held at the Bull,' said Mr Tewkesbury, 'which is the best thing I know about it, sir.'

'I see,' said Mr Wyndham, and began to wonder whether he was wise to have given a receipt in full. Perhaps he'd better mention the matter.

'There was one thing,' he began. 'My clerk tells me – '

'Take no notice, sir, no notice at all. I know barristers' clerks. They're worse than solicitors'. Disregard them, sir.

Forget them, sir. Take no notice of them whatever. Excuse me.' And Mr Tewkesbury refreshed himself again.

'What I wanted to mention, Mr Tewkesbury,' began Mr Wyndham again.

'There's nothing wrong with that brief, sir. Nothing wrong of any sort or kind whatsoever. I dictated the whole thing myself. Been doing it for years. You can't teach me how to dictate a brief, sir. If I may say so, sir, I've instructed the most exclusive counsel in my time – most exclusive. Sir Giles Farnaby – sir – before he became Attorney-General – I used to brief him regularly, sir, and once he said to me – these are his own words: "Mr Tewkesbury," he said, "your instructions are perfect." That's what he said, sir, perfect.'

'It wasn't about the brief itself – the instructions are admirable, if I may respectfully say so.'

It will be observed that Mr Wyndham, who would use the most unpardonable language to his opponents, witnesses and even judges, was always meek and humble to solicitors. They provided his bread and butter – or, to be more accurate, they provided a very small fraction of it. The balance came from a very small trust fund without which he certainly could not have remained at the Bar. But he was devoted to his profession, little as he understood its practice or its ethics, and even a drunken solicitor was treated by him with the greatest respect as long as it was humanly possible.

'Then what are you grumbling about?' asked Mr Tewkesbury. 'Excuse me.'

'It was just about the fee, as a matter of fact,' said Mr Wyndham.

Mr Tewkesbury finished what he was doing – and then turned on Mr Wyndham. 'About the fee, sir? About the fee? Let me tell you, sir, that F E Smith himself – the Right

Honourable Lord Birkenhead – would have been pleased to go to an inquest for fifty guineas. I've never seen such a fee, sir. Forty years I've been a solicitor – and never have I seen such a fee at an inquest. You're sure you're not mistaking this for one of your House of Lords cases or perhaps something in the Court of Appeal? Even there, sir, I've had counsel appearing for me for fifty guineas. Yes, sir, and for less, and pleased to do it, sir, and pleased to do it. Really, sir, I'd prefer you to criticise the brief rather than the fee. After all, everyone can make mistakes – I could have left something out of the brief – I didn't, but I could have – but the fee, sir – the fee – let me tell you, sir, it's the most magnificent fee I've ever seen counsel get at an inquest, and, no offence to you, sir, well-known counsel at that. Really, sir, I hope you're joking. It's beyond words. The fee. You must excuse me.'

'Oh – it's an excellent fee, I assure you, Mr Tewkesbury. Even if it hadn't been, I should never dream of complaining about a fee once my clerk had accepted the brief.'

'Then, suppose we have a little sleep,' said Mr Tewkesbury. 'We shan't be able to sleep at the inquest. Might as well get some in now. Forgive me, sir, but I was up late last night dictating briefs – which reminds me – I haven't quite decided to whom to send them. Difficult thing, these days, to find reliable counsel. D'you know anyone who knows anything about forgery, sir?'

'Well – as a matter of fact,' began Mr Wyndham, but Mr Tewkesbury interrupted.

'Forgive me, sir, I know what you're going to say. Weren't you in that forgery case some two or three years ago? A whole gang of them. They got about fifty years. Spread between them, of course. Fair shares for all.'

The only forgery case with which Mr Wyndham had been concerned (apart from the little matter of the receipt) was when he had devilled a plea of guilty at a Magistrates' Court for a waitress who had forged a reference. But it is difficult for counsel to recollect at once all the cases in which he has appeared and a little latitude must be allowed to him on such occasions.

'Let me think,' he began, 'did you say two or three years ago?'

'You're too modest, sir. Wasn't that the case where the judge complimented you on your address to the jury? "A model," didn't he call it?' Mr Wyndham's addresses to the jury had been called many things – even by his own clients sometimes – but a model was not one of them.

'Now, was there anything else you wanted to say, sir, before we have our little bit of shut-eye? I was wondering whether to mark the brief twenty-five or thirty guineas. In confidence, sir – I won't quote you, I assure you, sir, but it's so helpful to get it straight from counsel himself. You can't trust the clerks, sir, you can't really – they do their best for you, sir, of course, but you can't trust them, sir.'

Mr Tewkesbury shook his head sadly. 'Now, what would you say, sir, for a forgery case – twenty-five or thirty, sir? Would you look at it for twenty-five? I don't suppose you would, sir, I don't suppose you would. Very well, sir, I'll take your advice and thirty it shall be. And, after all, it's the client who pays, isn't it, and we don't give him credit. Oh – no, sir, not with crime. We get counsel's fee in first – we look after counsel first, sir …'

And then, realising that the subject he had raised was the one he had intended to avoid, he quickly stopped with one of his periodic: 'Excuse me's. 'And, now, I'm sorry, sir, but I shan't be fit for anything if I don't get some sleep. So please don't talk to me any more, sir, until we reach our destination. Good night to you, sir,' and murmuring 'Thirty it shall be,' Mr Tewkesbury at first pretended he was sleeping. Soon, however, his alcoholic snores made it quite plain that this was no pretence.

Mr Wyndham got out his brief and proceeded to make even more voluminous notes in the margin than he had already made. He also proceeded to underline further passages with various of his different coloured pencils, until at last almost every line of the brief had been underlined in at least one colour and often in two or even more. Had it been a civil action which had been compromised after brief delivered but long before the trial, no one could have said that Mr Wyndham had not read his brief. Whether he had understood it is another matter. Some of it, particularly Mr Tewkesbury's more florid passages, were, in fact, quite unintelligible.

'Counsel will observe,' ran one such passage, 'that this is not like the case of uneducated or illiterate [*sic*] people who do not know what they are doing. They knew very well what they were doing and counsel will please make the most of this. Counsel is respectfully requested to press this point home very hard. It is felt by your instructing solicitors that if this is done *in limine* it will do a great deal to get the Coroner on our side. Counsel will also please bear in mind the maxim *lex non cogit ad impossibilia* which seems to be very material in this case, but it is left to counsel's discretion how he uses this point.'

In dictating his instructions over a bottle of whisky, Mr Tewkesbury had in fact said anything which came into his head and which, from his point of view, rolled off his tongue comfortably.

Mr Wyndham continued to mark his brief but became increasingly disturbed by the snores of his instructing solicitor. Eventually: 'Shut up,' he said. He would not have dreamed of talking like that to a solicitor who was awake, but he felt satisfied that the sleeping Mr Tewkesbury would never know what he had said. Nothing happened at first.

'Shut up,' said Mr Wyndham, rather more loudly. The snoring stopped abruptly. Then: 'Thirty it shall be,' murmured Mr Tewkesbury and the snoring started all over again.

'Confound,' said Mr Wyndham, and tried to distract his own attention from the horrible noise by thinking about the briefs Mr Tewkesbury might send him as a result of this case. Bogg, Tewkesbury, he thought, I haven't heard of them before, but they seem to have the work all right. I really must make a big show with this case. This may be my chance. Perhaps there'll be a prosecution and I shall have made such an impression at the inquest that I'll be specially briefed for the Crown. After that, briefs would start pouring into his chambers. Forgery, murder, conspiracy to defraud, manslaughter – everything. As a prosecutor he would become known as 'The terror of the cosh boys.' He could see himself pointing a finger at the prisoner giving evidence and asking his last question in cross-examination: 'In the face of that, do you dare to stand there and tell my Lord and the jury that you are not guilty?' There would be no reply. The prisoner would moisten his lips, but no sound would come. He would repeat the question. Still no answer. 'Very well,' he would say, 'I will not press that question. The jury have heard the only answer you can give – none!' But as defending counsel he would become another Marshall Hall. 'He must have a chance,' people would say, even when the prisoner's guilt seemed obvious. 'Frith Wyndham's appearing for him.' He would take silk.

'Do you move, Mr Wyndham?' – or, perhaps even by then, 'Do you move, Sir Frith?' And then, perhaps, one day, one great day, he would be made a judge – perhaps even Lord Chief Justice. He could hear himself presiding in the Court of Criminal Appeal. 'There is nothing in this appeal and it will be dismissed.' That was what had been said to him on the only occasion when he had appeared in that Court. One or two other things had been said to him on that occasion, too, but mercifully his memory for such matters was short. Yes, perhaps this was his chance. He must do himself justice. And then, apart from anything else, there were these other briefs which Mr Tewkesbury had dangled in front of him. It never occurred to him that they did not exist and that, if they had existed, they would not have come his way. Forgery. The forger's den. There was almost a romantic sound about it. And thirty guineas, too, even twenty-five – and possibly several refreshers. A forgery case would take some time. Perhaps a week. Five, six refreshers. Certainly not less than four. Ten guineas a time. His figures for the year would equal the last three years put together before he'd finished. And then there were the other briefs Mr Tewkesbury had mentioned. He wondered what they were. Not likely to be murder or he'd have read about it. False pretences perhaps. That usually took a long time. Bigamy, perjury, assault occasioning actual bodily harm, bathing in the Serpentine in prohibited hours. Things began to get a little confused in Mr Wyndham's mind. He was Lord Chief Justice, he was defending Mr Tewkesbury, he was prosecuting Mr Tewkesbury, he was taking silk, receiving large cheques, giving a receipt for a cheque he hadn't had, interviewing a prisoner in the condemned cell, in the condemned cell himself, sitting as judge at the Old Bailey, picking up the nosegay and then throwing it playfully to a pretty girl

177

barrister. No, this won't do – he must wake up. And, with an effort, he did. Mr Tewkesbury was still snoring, and, when the train stopped, he found that they were already two stations past Pemberton.

CHAPTER EIGHTEEN

The Inquest

'Really,' said Mr Tewkesbury. 'Really, sir, this is, if I may say so, a pretty bad beginning. We shall require a car, sir, or we shall be late.'

'I'm so sorry,' said Mr Wyndham. 'I'm afraid I fell asleep.'

'I very much hope, sir,' said Mr Tewkesbury severely, 'that you will not repeat the performance at the inquest. Excuse me.'

At a cost of three pounds they hired a car. Little was said on the journey. Mr Tewkesbury was dozing, and Mr Wyndham was wondering how he could avoid paying for the car. After all, it was as much Mr Tewkesbury's fault as his. He rehearsed little speeches to himself – about sharing the cost – even tossing for it – that would give him an even chance, at any rate – or perhaps Mr Tewkesbury would say: 'The client will pay, sir, the client will pay.' That really was the answer. Or, alternatively, if the worst came to the worst, he could say he had no money on him or not sufficient. But, had he been a worthier opponent of Mr Tewkesbury, he would have found it a hopeless task. Mr Tewkesbury was an expert in these matters. As soon as they arrived at the Bull and Mr Wyndham had awakened him, he got out and walked towards the entrance to the Bull saying as he went: 'Just pay the driver, my dear sir, please.

179

I've no small change. The client will reimburse you.' And then, from the door, he turned round. 'Hurry up, my dear sir. We're late already.'

The Coroner's Court is probably the oldest Court in England. Although its rules have recently been revised, they are still the most flexible of any Court and rightly so. The Coroner is not bound by the rules of evidence, and, therefore, he can pursue his enquiries as to the cause of death – which, in death cases, is his main duty – without the restrictions to which other Courts are rightly subject. Were his conduct of the proceedings circumscribed by rules of evidence, much important matter might be excluded. It must be borne in mind, too, that no person's guilt or innocence or civil liability depends upon the finding of the Coroner or his jury, though, of course, his reputation may be affected by what happens at an inquest. If a prosecution is taking place, the inquest will in most cases be postponed until the prosecution is over. Where there has been no prosecution prior to the conclusion of the inquest, it is true that the verdict of the Coroner's jury may result in there being a prosecution or, indeed, may influence the police or Director of Public Prosecutions not to launch a prosecution. But, inasmuch as the verdict may affect a person's reputation and because it may partly be based on hearsay, most Coroners are extremely careful to see that no one concerned is unfairly prejudiced. Indeed, in street accident cases, many Coroners and many Coroner's juries seem to go out of their way to come to the rescue of the poor driver who has driven his vehicle, weighing anything from half a ton upwards, into a pedestrian. 'It must be terrible for him having killed someone. Poor fellow,' say the jury, and exonerate him from all blame.

The inquest was being held in the lounge of the Bull which was far too small for the large number of people who wanted to be present. In consequence it was crammed to overflowing, and the disappointed overflow clustered round the porch, making access to the lounge something of a problem for Mr Tewkesbury and Mr Wyndham, who nevertheless managed to reach the door. This opened sufficiently to enable them to edge in along the wall behind a solid row of standing people. The Coroner had arrived (indeed, he had been told that counsel was coming and he had been waiting to see who it would be) and the jury were in their places. Every seat in the lounge was taken and, apart from a small space on one side of the Coroner's table which had been kept free as a witness box, almost every available inch of floor space was occupied. Mr Tewkesbury, using Mr Wyndham as a kind of snowplough, managed somehow to open a gap through which they both moved forward until Mr Wyndham judged that he was near enough to the Coroner to remark (as he did) in a loud voice: 'Where are the seats for counsel?'

'Are you appearing in this case?' asked the Coroner.

'I am, sir.'

'Your name, please?'

'Frith Wyndham, counsel instructed by Messrs Bogg, Tewkesbury and Company.'

'And whom do you represent, please?'

'The next-of-kin.'

'I beg your pardon?' said the Coroner. The police had already ascertained that Sidney had been living with Martha, that they were not married and that, as far as could be ascertained, he had no relatives – none at any rate who were prepared to admit it. They had also ascertained that there were several officers from the

Criminal Investigation Department who could identify him and one was present for the purpose.

'The next-of-kin,' repeated Mr Wyndham.

'And the name and relationship, please,' asked the Coroner.

'I've never been asked such a question before,' said Mr Wyndham, who had no idea what the name of his client was.

'Well, you are now,' said the Coroner pleasantly. 'Would you mind letting me have it and then we can get on. We've waited twenty minutes for you already.'

'What's the name of the client?' whispered Mr Wyndham to Mr Tewkesbury, who was not asleep as he had to stand up.

'No idea,' said Mr Tewkesbury. 'You should have asked me in the train if you'd wanted to know.'

'If you don't know now, you couldn't have known then,' said Mr Wyndham.

'I could have found out,' said Mr Tewkesbury.

It was useless for Mr Wyndham to go on arguing or to point out that he could not have found out, either on the train or during their car journey, so he turned again to the Coroner.

'If you'd just put down "the next-of-kin," sir, I'd be much obliged,' he said.

'But I've been told there aren't any,' said the Coroner. 'So far, you appear to confirm that.' Then he added: 'I suppose you don't happen to be appearing for a lady called Mrs York, do you?'

Mr Wyndham turned to Mr Tewkesbury.

'That'll do as well as any other,' said Mr Tewkesbury. He was already bored with the proceedings. He wanted to sit down, or, if he had to stand up, to have a drink, and he couldn't do either.

'Yes, sir, that is the lady's name.'

'Oh, very well,' said the Coroner. 'I'll stretch a point and let you appear for her. But, really, you know, you've no *locus standi.*'

'Really, sir?' said Mr Wyndham. 'I have a right to appear. I claim the right of counsel to represent his client.'

'Well, we won't argue about it – Mr – Mr – Mr – ?'

'Wyndham.'

'Mr Wyndham, because I'm going to let you appear, but you haven't in fact any right to do so.'

'Am I going to be allowed to sit down?' asked Mr Wyndham.

'Certainly,' said the Coroner, 'if you can find a seat. That's the trouble with being late. The best seats get taken quickly.'

'I apologise for our being late, sir. Unfortunately, we were carried on by the train.'

'Very well,' said the Coroner. 'Now, let's get on.'

'But I can't represent my client like this,' said Mr Wyndham. And, indeed, there was a good deal to be said for his complaint. He was wedged in a crowd of people, with his brief in one hand and *Stone's Justices' Manual* in the other.

'Oh, dear,' said the Coroner. 'It's such a pity you weren't in time. Could one of the gentlemen of the press let you share his chair perhaps? Oh – thank you very much, Mr Munro. If you can make your way over there, you can share Mr Munro's chair.'

'What about me?' said Mr Tewkesbury. He was determined to get to sleep again if it was humanly possible.

'I'm afraid that's the best we can do,' said the Coroner. 'But the proceedings won't take very long. So I hope you won't be too uncomfortable.'

Instead of replying, Mr Tewkesbury pushed his way after Mr Wyndham and caught him by the arm. 'Speak up for me,' he said. 'That's what you're paid for, isn't it? Get me a chair.'

The opening of the inquest was very different from what poor Mr Wyndham had imagined. He had thought of himself sitting comfortably behind a green baize table and, in effect, having command of the proceedings. Instead, he had been invited to share the arm of a chair. And now it looked as though he would have to give even that up to his instructing solicitor.

'Go on, speak up,' said Mr Tewkesbury.

'Could my solicitor have a chair, too, please?' asked Mr Wyndham, not very happily.

'Really,' said the Coroner, 'this is getting tiresome. I'm afraid you'll have to make do with what you have.'

'I've never been treated like this before,' said Mr Wyndham.

'I hope you haven't been late before,' said the Coroner.

'You'll be standing up anyway,' said Mr Tewkesbury. 'I'll take this. You stand in front.'

So the unfortunate Mr Wyndham, brief still in the one hand and *Stone's Justices' Manual* still in the other, stood in front of Mr Tewkesbury, who flopped down on the arm of the chair in which Mr Munro was sitting. Mr Munro had had a good deal of experience of whisky, but the fumes from Mr Tewkesbury were more than even he could bear. He sat up suddenly and drove his elbow so hard into Mr Tewkesbury that he slipped off the arm and collapsed on the floor. There he would have remained, quite happily. It was far more comfortable than the arm. But unkind arms insisted on lifting him up again, in spite of his muttered: 'Leave me alone.' As soon as he was on his feet again, he whispered to Mr Wyndham: 'You get on with it. I'll be next door, if you want me,' and elbowed his way through the crowd towards the door marked 'Bar.' It was locked. Mr Tewkesbury rattled the handle, but to no purpose.

'Now, please,' said the Coroner, 'I want to get on.'

'Silence,' said the Coroner's officer. Mr Tewkesbury remained standing, kept on his feet only by the press of people against him.

At last the jury were duly sworn and the Coroner addressed them.

'This is an inquest on an unfortunate man who was going under the name of Sidney York, but I think you'll find his real name was Brown. He was found dead at the bottom of the back stairs of this inn and had obviously fallen down them. Call Mr Cumberland, please.'

Mr Cumberland went into the witness box and took the oath. He said that he was the licensee of the inn and described how he had heard the fall and found Sidney dead at the bottom of the back stairs. He stated that a room had been booked for him in the name, of Sidney York.

'That's all, thank you,' said the Coroner. 'Now Detective Sergeant Gage.'

'But I want to cross-examine the witness,' said Mr Wyndham.

'I dare say,' said the Coroner, 'but it won't be necessary. Unless, of course, you're disputing what the witness has so far said. Are you?'

'No,' said Mr Wyndham, 'but there are numerous other facts I want to elicit. I shall be a long time cross-examining this witness.'

'There you are mistaken,' said the Coroner. 'You won't be any time at all at the moment. Later on, if necessary, the witness can be recalled.'

'This is an outrage, sir,' protested Mr Wyndham. 'I am a barrister of many years' standing and never in the whole of my professional career – '

'Be quiet, Mr Wyndham, please. I'm in charge of the proceedings here. No injustice will be done to your client, for whom, as I have already pointed out, you are only allowed to appear as an act of grace. You have no right to be here at all.'

'No right, sir?' said Mr Wyndham, angrily. 'I have every right. Perhaps you haven't read the new Coroners' rules? You no longer have the right to throw people out of your Court irrespective of justice.'

'I know the rules, thank you, Mr Wyndham. I don't want to be unkind to your client. So I will only repeat that you have no right to be here at all. But I must ask you to comply with my rulings. Otherwise I shall have to ask you to go.'

'Under protest,' said Mr Wyndham, 'I shall comply, but I must request you to make a note of my objection, and of my desire to cross-examine the witness and your refusal to let me. He is a most important witness. How you imagine justice can be done – '

'Now, Mr Wyndham, I'm being very patient. I don't want to have you put out, so please be quiet.'

Mr Wyndham could not subside, as he was too firmly wedged between the people next to him and someone else had already taken the arm of Mr Munro's chair. He remained standing uncomfortably and thinking, with regret, how differently the proceedings were going from what he had imagined in his daydream in the train. At this rate it was unlikely – even in his own view – that he would become Lord Chief Justice. He felt that there was something else he ought to do, but he could not even make a dignified withdrawal from the room; he was too hemmed in. And, anyway, he hoped to get a chance of asking someone some questions. But it was all a long way removed from 'Sir Frith, do you move?' or 'Frith Wyndham's speech for the defence. Latest.' Across the room he saw Mr Tewkesbury's expressionless face against the door of the bar. His eyes were closed. He was asleep. It was the first time he had been able to do this standing without an accident. His little affair with the bicycle had occurred owing to his going to sleep while riding it.

Detective Sergeant Gage then gave evidence of identification. The dead man, he said, had been going under the name of Sidney York, but his real name was Brown. As far as could be ascertained, he had no relations. He was living with a woman who was known as Mrs York, but she was not his wife. The Coroner interposed to say to the jury that the object of this evidence was not to blacken the character of the deceased or the lady called Mrs York or to cause her pain, but, as far as could be discovered the only methods of identifying the deceased were his photographs at Scotland Yard and the evidence of officers there who knew him.

'Now, Dr Salthouse, please,' said the Coroner.

'Am I not to be allowed to cross-examine any of the witnesses?' asked Mr Wyndham.

'Not at the moment, Mr Wyndham, unless you dispute their evidence.'

'But there's a great deal about the dead man I want to elicit. My instructions are that he had certain information – '

'Be quiet, Mr Wyndham,' said the Coroner sternly. 'If you interrupt any more, I really shall have you removed. You will have every opportunity of cross-examining the witnesses if it becomes necessary.'

Mr Wyndham was about to expostulate again, but he realised that the Coroner meant what he said, and, though he would get into the papers if he were thrown out, it was not exactly the kind of advertisement he wanted, though it would, no doubt, be better than none. So he decided to reserve his final row with the Coroner for later.

Dr Salthouse, the pathologist, then went into the box and was sworn. After giving his qualifications, he said that he had performed a post-mortem on the body of the dead man. He was aged about sixty and the body was well nourished for a man of that age who appeared to be a chronic alcoholic.

'I found,' went on the doctor, 'a fractured vertebra consistent with a fall downstairs. Round the site of the fracture, however, there was no haemorrhage. I discovered the reason for this, which was that there was a fresh ante-mortem clot blocking one of the main coronary arteries of the heart. It is plain, therefore, that death was due not to the fractured vertebra but to coronary thrombosis. The vertebra was fractured after death. Hence the absence of haemorrhage. The deceased had an enlarged and fatty liver and there was quite an amount of alcohol in the stomach. The cause of the condition of the liver was, in all probability, chronic alcoholism, as I could find no other condition in the body which would have accounted for it.'

'Do you consider that the fall downstairs of which we have heard had any connection with the death of the deceased?' asked the Coroner.

'None whatever,' said the doctor. 'In my opinion he must have died before he fell.'

'Now, Mr Wyndham,' said the Coroner, 'would you like to ask this witness any questions?'

Even when carefully briefed by an expert, it is not always easy for counsel to cross-examine professional witnesses on medical, scientific and technical matters. Mr Wyndham, even if so instructed, would have made a very poor job of it. As it was, however, he had no instructions at all. Everyone had assumed that Sidney had been killed by the fall. However, here was an opportunity to show what he could do and Mr Wyndham prepared to do battle with the doctor.

'Are you quite certain of your conclusions, doctor?' was his first question.

'Quite,' said the doctor.

'Why?' asked Mr Wyndham.

'Because I conducted the post-mortem.'

'May you not have made a mistake?'

'In what respect, may I ask?'

'In any respect.'

'We can all make mistakes, but I can only say that I carefully examined the organs to which I have referred and my findings are as I have stated. There was certainly no doubt about two things – there was a clot in one of the main arteries and there was no haemorrhage at the site of the fractured vertebra.'

Although Mr Wyndham had no intention of sitting down, or rather of ceasing his cross-examination, he would have liked to turn round to Mr Tewkesbury and ask him if he had any question to suggest. As it was, Mr Tewkesbury was at the far end of the room asleep. Even, however, if he had been behind him and awake, the only kind of advice he would have been likely to receive from him would have been: 'Tell him he's a liar' or 'Ask him why he didn't say it before.' Neither suggestion would have been very helpful. For a moment Mr Wyndham, in his discomfort, wondered whether he could make signs to Mr Tewkesbury like a tic-tac man at a racecourse, but two things made this impossible. Mr Wyndham knew no code and Mr Tewkesbury's eyes were closed. Mr Wyndham paused so long that, as he could not sit down to indicate that he had finished, the Coroner said: 'Is that all you wish to ask, Mr Wyndham?'

'By no means,' said Mr Wyndham, 'but I have rather been taken by surprise by this evidence, and I want to test it.'

'Your next question, then, please,' said the Coroner.

'Why did you say he died before he fell?'

'I have just told you. There was no haemorrhage at the site of the fracture. Had he been alive when he fell, there would have been some haemorrhage there.'

'Are you sure of that?'

'Yes – quite sure.'

'Why?'

'Because it is an established medical fact.'

'I suggest it isn't.'

'I can't stop you suggesting it isn't, but it is, as any medically qualified man knows. And, indeed, a good many students too,' he added.

'There's no doubt this man fell down and broke his neck, is there?'

'None at all from what I have heard and from what I saw of the body.'

'You don't suggest he already had a broken neck before he fell, I suppose?'

'I certainly don't. On the contrary, I have just agreed with you that I personally have no doubt that he broke his neck when he fell.'

'If a man breaks his neck, it usually kills him, doesn't it?'

'Yes, usually.'

'This man broke his neck, didn't he?'

'Yes.'

'Well, it killed him then, didn't it?'

'Isn't there something of an undistributed middle about that question?' interposed the Coroner.

'I beg your pardon?' asked Mr Wyndham, quite mystified.

'Never mind,' said the Coroner. 'Any more questions?'

'I'd like that one answered first,' said Mr Wyndham.

'What was the question?'

'It was the broken neck which killed him, wasn't it?'

'No.'

'Why not?'

'Because he was already dead.'

'Do you say that, if the light had been on, he would still have fallen?'

'I certainly do.'

'Why?'

'Because he was dead. And, being dead, he couldn't have remained at the top of the staircase. He would have fallen down it – as he did.'

'I suggest to you that, if the light had been on, the deceased would have been alive today, and his unfortunate widow – the lady I represent – would not be in mourning now?'

The doctor said nothing, but gave a gentle sigh.

'Well, sir, will you not answer my question?' thundered Mr Wyndham in his most powerful voice, very different from the one he had used to Mr Tewkesbury in the train. It reverberated to such an extent round the room that it half woke up Mr Tewkesbury, who murmured: 'I've no small change,' and went to sleep again.

'I thought I had – at least twice,' said the doctor in a resigned voice. 'But what is it this time?'

'How dare you speak to me like that,' shouted Mr Wyndham, with the result that Mr Tewkesbury murmured: 'None at all!'

'I ask for your protection, sir,' went on Mr Wyndham, turning his head – he could not move his body – to the Coroner.

'Protection against what, Mr Wyndham?'

'Being insulted – grossly insulted.'

'I don't think any insult was intended,' said the Coroner. 'Please continue.'

'Well, sir?' said Mr Wyndham. 'What have you to say to that?'

'To what?'

'Really! This is beyond bearing. If the light had been on, would not the deceased have been alive and well today?'

'If the light had been on,' answered the doctor, 'the deceased would have been just as dead as he is today – no more – no less.'

'Really, doctor, I think – ' said the Coroner, mildly reproving the witness.

'Thank you, sir,' said Mr Wyndham, 'but I'm not going to be browbeaten by you, doctor. You may think it amusing that a man is dead. But let me tell you that it is not in the least amusing to his poor widow – to the lady I represent – or to his friends and relations.'

'Well, really,' said the witness, 'I'm the last person to be unkind about the dead, but, having seen the body and heard the evidence I should say that this man's death was a happy release for everyone. He died as one would have expected him to die. If he hadn't had a thrombus – a clot that is – he'd have probably had a cerebral haemorrhage. He died instantaneously. He did very well for himself in the circumstances.'

'This isn't a memorial service,' said Mr Wyndham, 'but an inquest to ascertain the cause of death and I suggest to you that death was caused by the absence of a light and I shall go on to suggest to the other witnesses, when I'm allowed to do so, that the reason there was no light was because – '

But the Coroner interrupted.

'I have allowed you considerable latitude, Mr Wyndham. You will kindly confine your questions to those which are material to this witness' evidence. I will not have counsel trying to make a speech under the guise of asking questions. Is there anything more which you want to ask this witness?'

'But I'm not allowed to cross-examine the witnesses who have already been called and, if no other witnesses are going to be called, there's no one else of whom to ask the questions.'

'I'm not here to argue with you,' said the Coroner, 'but I don't mind dealing with your last observation. If, as the witness says, death took place before the man fell, the presence or absence of a light and the reason for its absence, if it was absent, are wholly irrelevant to this enquiry. That is why I invited you to cross-examine this witness first. If there were a doubt as to the cause of death, the position would be different. I may tell you that, had I had the result of the post-mortem examination before I summoned the jury, I should not have summoned one. It did appear in the first instance, until the results of the post-mortem were known, that death might have been due to an accident and I have had a number of statements taken in that connection. Now, however, if Dr Salthouse's evidence remains unchallenged, that is an end of the matter.'

'Well, I challenge Dr Salthouse's evidence,' said Mr Wyndham.

'Are there any further relevant questions you wish to ask him?'

Mr Wyndham instinctively looked behind him, forgetting for the moment that his instructing solicitor was elsewhere.

'I don't think there is any point in my asking any more.'

'Very well, then,' said the Coroner. 'I take it there is no evidence – no medical evidence which you wish to tender.'

'No, sir,' said Mr Wyndham.

'Well, that concludes the case, members of the jury. There is really no need for me to address you on the matter. You heard the doctor's evidence and I assume that you will return a verdict in accordance with his evidence.'

The jury duly returned a verdict that death was due to natural causes, namely coronary thrombosis.

Immediately afterwards Colonel Brain, who was extremely disappointed at not having been called to give evidence, met the reporter Cyril outside the Bull.

'Now, my dear fellow,' said the colonel, 'I'm prepared to be pumped. Indeed, I'm almost overflowing as it is. It's really too bad. I'd taken a great deal of trouble over my evidence. However, old Archie Preston knows what he's doing. But, if it had been a Court of Enquiry in my battalion, it wouldn't have happened like that. We used to take a long time and hear all the witnesses before we exonerated the fellow.'

'Oh, well,' said Cyril, 'there doesn't seem much point now, but, if you'd care to tell me about that coincidence, I'd listen.'

So the colonel told him about his conversation with James and Judy just after the lunatic had attacked him. This information shook Cyril considerably.

'They've had a bit of luck, haven't they?'

'Oh – I don't know about luck, my dear fellow. You've too suspicious a mind. As a matter of fact, I could tell you something else that would shake you. I wouldn't have breathed a word about it before the inquest, but, now it's all over, it doesn't matter.'

'What's that?'

The colonel then told Cyril about the incident with Judy's bag, when James had suddenly driven off with it. 'You know, my dear fellow, if I'd been a suspicious person I'd have said the lamp was inside that bag. I expect that's what you think now, isn't it? But it doesn't matter what you think, does it, because he died of natural causes – same as we all hope to one day, my dear fellow.'

Later that day Cyril reported this conversation to Mr Bean and was amazed to see the effect it had on him.

'One more link,' said Mr Bean, 'and we've got them.'

'Got them?' said Cyril. 'But he died of natural causes. I don't understand.'

'Perhaps you wouldn't, but have you never heard of attempted murder or conspiracy to murder?'

'But how can you attempt to murder a man who just dies?'

'Just think,' said Mr Bean. 'Supposing a man tries to pick your pocket and you've got nothing in it. He's not guilty of stealing, because there was nothing to steal, but would you say he was guilty of nothing if you found his hand in your pocket? Supposing you shot at a man, and he happened to die of natural causes before the bullet reached him. You wouldn't be hanged for it, but you would go to prison for a nice long time for attempted murder, wouldn't you? That's what's happened here. And quite good enough for me. Now, I'm going up to town to see Mrs York again. You stay here. I may want you later. I wonder if we can show that they were all three in it – but that's too good to expect.'

CHAPTER NINETEEN

Solicitor and Counsel

'Did you think there was anything else I could do?' asked Mr Wyndham anxiously of Mr Tewkesbury on the way back in the train.

'Do, sir? Anything else you could do, sir? Nothing, sir. It was a magnificent performance, if I may say so, sir. I congratulate you. What was the verdict, did you say?'

'Natural causes.'

'Natural causes, eh? Well, juries are funny things, you know, most unreliable. A man falls down the stairs and breaks his neck and they say it's natural. Well – perhaps it was natural for him – perhaps he was an acrobat or a comedian, sir.'

'It was the doctor's evidence which did it.'

'Professional witness, sir. Take no notice of them, sir, disregard them, sir. They say anything. But it doesn't surprise me, sir. I'm surprised I didn't hear it, though. The doctor said that breaking one's neck falling downstairs was natural, did he? I should like to have heard that. I wasn't in a good part of the room for hearing, sir. I'm sorry I wasn't able to be more support to you, sir, but I thought yours was a magnificent performance, sir. You must have fried that doctor, sir. You wouldn't let him get away with nonsense like that, sir. You ate him alive I expect, sir. He'll respect you, sir, for that, however much he may have disliked you at the time. Mark my words, sir, he'll respect you. And, now, if you'll excuse me, sir. I've had rather a trying day.'

He took a generous pull at the flask and settled down for a sleep.

'Well, there's one thing about going back. They'll turn us out at the other end. Can't go two stations beyond this time.'

'Would you like the brief back now, Mr Tewkesbury, or will you send for it when you send down the balance of the fee?' asked Mr Wyndham.

'What's that you said, sir? Balance of the fee. I don't understand, sir. My firm always pay counsel in advance in such cases. As I told you before, sir, counsel comes first with us. And in case your clerk should make a mistake, sir, we take a receipt, sir, we take a receipt. And in criminal work, sir – and we count an inquest as criminal work – we pay in cash, sir, cash – not by cheque. I take it, if I may mention such a thing, sir, that you were paid in cash?'

'Well – yes – ' began Mr Wyndham.

'As I said, sir, I'm glad there was no mistake. Now a receipt's an important document, sir, and we keep receipts, sir. Because if counsel gives a receipt saying he's received a sum of money – he's received that sum of money. Counsel's receipt is as good as the Bank of England, sir. It's respected, sir. And why is it respected? Because, sir, because no barrister would give a receipt for shall we say fifty guineas, sir – just as an example – sir – unless he'd received fifty guineas. And why wouldn't he, sir – because it would be unprofessional, sir, and he might be disbarred for doing such a thing, sir. Of course, in spite of that there are a few such men in the Temple, sir, I'm told – some black sheep in every fold – but my firm would never go to chambers of that kind, sir. We're a little old-fashioned maybe, sir, but we like to stick to the rules, sir. Honesty, sir, and straightforwardness, sir, we find the best policy. And I'll tell you another thing, sir, in case you're still worried about some mistake your clerk may have made. D'you know what forgery is, sir? I've remembered it from the day I took my solicitors' final, and that's going back a bit, sir. Forgery is making a false document with intent that it should be used as genuine, sir. Now, sir, if you gave me, say ten pounds and I gave you a receipt for, say, twenty pounds, that would be forgery, sir, and a party to such a thing I would not be, sir, positively I would not be a party to such a thing. Nor, sir, I am quite sure, would you, sir. I wouldn't insult you by asking the question, sir. Indeed, sir, if I were a younger man and I asked you such a question, I should expect you to strike me, sir, yes, sir, and I should deserve it. Now, what was it you were saying, sir?'

'It doesn't matter, thank you,' said Mr Wyndham and very nearly burst into tears.

'Well, in that case, sir, I'll bid you a very good night, sir, and thank you very much for your services, sir, though I think you'd be the first to agree that they were handsomely paid for, sir. Excuse me.'

Meantime, Mr Bean was hurrying up to London to see Mrs York. As soon as he found her, he told her the result of the inquest and gave her £10. The lady was delighted.

'There's one question I want to ask you,' said Bean, after he had waved aside the lady's thanks. 'D'you know why Mr York went down to Murrell Keeping and stayed at the Bull?'

'He had a telegram.'

'You don't happen still to have it, do you?'

'I'll look.' Mrs York did look and she found it.

'May I keep it? Thank you so much. And I dare say you'll have some extra expenses now. Please take this.' And he gave her another £10.

Mr Bean then returned to Pemberton and asked for an interview with the Police Superintendent. He then presented to that surprised police officer a most formidable case against James and Judy. With some extra evidence to show that the lamp had been in Judy's bag when taken away by James, it seemed an open and shut case of attempt or conspiracy to murder or both. If it could be proved that the lamp was in Judy's bag, the case against them was as follows:

1. The deceased had some story about their father which he had suggested selling to the *Clarion*.

2. It was obviously a matter of sufficient importance for them to wire to him to come to the Bull.

3. Colonel Brain had suggested to them that a method of killing anyone you wanted to get rid of was to ask him to the Bull and take the lamp out.

4. The deceased came to the Bull.

5. Mr Cumberland was sure he had left the bulb in position in the socket, but it was not there at the time of the fall and had disappeared.

6. (If it could be proved) James had taken away that very bulb in Judy's bag.

7. Judy had been frightened when asked by one of Mr Bean's reporters if she knew anything about the lamp.

'If that isn't attempted murder,' said Mr Bean, 'I don't know what is.'

'I'll have to consider these statements,' said the Superintendent. 'I think they may require some explanation.'

'I'll say they do,' said Mr Bean.

'Don't be too sure,' said the Superintendent. 'Attempted murder is a very serious charge, and the son and daughter of a judge are not the sort of people to commit it.'

'They might to keep their father out of trouble. I saw this fellow. He was a nasty piece of work all right. A real blackmailer, if ever there was one.'

'Then, if I may say so, sir. I don't quite understand why you take such an interest, not to say pleasure, in piecing together a case against them. Naturally I have my duty to do, however unpleasant, and I shall do it. But if this man was a blackmailer – and you seem to be satisfied of that – and if a man's children tried to put him out of the way – well, the law's the law – we all know that – but I know where my sympathies would be.'

'Have you ever been in the witness box, Superintendent?'

'Many times.'

'Before Mr Justice Beverley by any chance?'

'Once, as matter of fact, sir.'

'Was he nice to you?'

'As a matter of fact – he was, sir. He made a recommendation about me.'

'Well – that accounts for a difference in our point of view, Superintendent. I also appeared in the witness box before him – but he didn't recommend me.'

'Well – sir, there's nothing illegal in piecing a case together out of spite, but that's what it seems to me you're doing. I'm sorry that I've anything to do with it. But you're quite right – the case is much too strong not to be investigated at the least. So I shall go into it thoroughly, sir. But I must say that I'm surprised at a man of your stature stooping so low. Good evening, sir.' And the Superintendent got up and showed Mr Bean the door.

'I shall report you for that remark, Superintendent.'

'You can report what you like, sir. I also shall make a full report of how and why you chose to take so prominent a part in this enquiry.'

And the Superintendent shut the door in his face.

Mr Bean left the police station a very angry man. His hatred of Mr Justice Beverley was now diverted temporarily at any rate to the Superintendent. He shall be reduced to a policeman, he said to himself. Reduced to the ranks. But even had he been the type of megalomaniac who kills, he would not have killed the Superintendent. He wanted to see him abased, crushed. He should learn that you cannot talk to Alexander Bean in that way and not regret it for the rest of your life. But how to get even with him? That was in some ways a greater problem than that of getting even with the judge. Well – he would sleep on it. But something should be done.

That same evening the judge's household were feeling much more cheerful about things. They said little, but the verdict had been a great relief, and almost as great a relief was the fact that the medical evidence made it unnecessary to call either James, Judy or Colonel Brain as witnesses. The inquest could not have gone better.

All Judy had said was to Bernard: 'It'll be all right now, won't it?'

'Yes, I think so,' he replied.

Similarly James had said to his father: 'Will anything more happen now, d'you think?'

'One can't be sure. These reporters around the place may mean anything or nothing.'

And then came a ring at the bell. It was the Superintendent with a Detective-Inspector and Colonel Brain.

CHAPTER TWENTY

The Caution

The Superintendent asked to see the judge.

'I'm extremely sorry to trouble you, Sir John, at this time of day, but I'm afraid my business is urgent.'

'I quite understand,' said the judge. 'What is it you want?'

'It's regarding the death of Sidney York, I'm afraid. I should like to ask your son and daughter a few questions and you too, Sir John, if I may.'

'Very well. I'll send for them. Mr Kent, the Assistant Commissioner, is also here. I take it you've no objection to his being present.'

'Of course not, sir.'

So James and Judy and Bernard were sent for by the judge.

'Do you mind my asking the questions, sir?' asked the Superintendent of Bernard. 'Or would you prefer me to tell you what it's all about first?'

'No,' said Bernard. 'You ask what you want. For the moment, treat me as a private individual – who happens to be engaged to Miss Beverley.'

This was a shock for the Superintendent. But there was nothing to be done about it. Since he had joined the police force, he had always plodded steadily ahead. He never had any difficulty in recognising where his duty lay, however unpleasant it might be. This was the most embarrassing moment he had ever experienced, but the job had to be done.

'Colonel Brain here tells me,' he began eventually, 'that shortly before Sidney York died, he made a jocular suggestion to you, Mr Beverley and Miss Beverley, as to how to kill a man. May I ask is that correct?'

'I'd no idea,' put in Colonel Brain, 'that I was going to cause all this trouble. When the Superintendent came to me, I told him it was just nonsense. I'm most terribly sorry.'

'Yes,' said James. 'It is correct.'

'And the method he suggested was – '

'Jocularly,' put in the colonel.

'Yes, jocularly,' went on the Superintendent, 'was to ask a man to stay at the Bull for the night and take the back staircase lamp out. Is that right too, may I ask?'

'Yes,' said James.

'Did you in fact invite Sidney York to stay the night at the Bull?'

'Yes.'

'For what purpose?'

'To sign an agreement.'

'May I ask the object of the agreement?'

'I'm not prepared to say in detail, but he was being a nuisance and I wanted him to agree to keep away from us.'

'Was he being a grave nuisance to you, sir?'

James hesitated. Then: 'Yes, he was,' he said.

'Is it a great relief to you that he's dead?'

Again slight hesitation by James and then again: 'Yes, it is.'

'You know, don't you, that the lamp by the back stairs was missing from the Bull immediately after he fell down the stairs?'

'I have been told so.'

'Do you know where that lamp is?'

James hesitated much longer this time. Then: 'No,' he said.

Sir John shifted uncomfortably in his chair. If James was going to lie about it, ought he to intervene? His last statement might just be true, as the lamp might have been found and moved again, but this was unlikely, and James' statement was as near a lie as made no difference.

'Colonel Brain says that immediately after the accident you took away Miss Beverley's handbag. Mr Beverley, was the lamp in that handbag?'

'No,' said James. 'It was not.'

He had had to make a quick decision, and, although it was no longer a case of life and death, James knew that, if a charge of attempted murder were made against Judy, it would be the end – not only for her but for all of them. The same thoughts had gone through the judge's mind, but he, too, had made a decision.

'Will you excuse me a moment, Superintendent?' he said. 'I want to speak to my son before he goes on answering your questions.'

'Certainly, sir.'

The judge went out of the room with James. They came back after a few minutes.

'I want to correct that last statement,' said James. 'The lamp was in the bag.'

The Superintendent paused.

'Then I'm afraid,' he said, after some slight hesitation, 'that I shall have to warn you both, Mr Beverley, and you, Miss Beverley, that you need not answer any further questions if you do not wish to do so, but that, if you do, your answers may be used in evidence if a charge is made against you.'

'Have you then made up your mind to prefer a charge, Superintendent?' asked the judge.

'I shall have to refer the matter to the Director, Sir John, and follow his instructions, but, in view of the evidence which I had, I felt it only right to administer a caution before proceeding further. I think you should know that I have a statement from Mr Cumberland that he definitely remembers putting the lamp back not long before the accident.'

'I shouldn't rely too much on what he says, my dear fellow,' said Colonel Brain. 'He can't remember his own Christian names sometimes.'

'I'm sorry,' said the Superintendent. 'Desperately sorry, if I may say so, but there's no getting away from the fact that there appears to be a very substantial body of evidence. In view of all the circumstances, I feel it right that I should consult the Director before a charge is preferred, but I'm bound to say that I shall be surprised if he does not instruct me to prefer one.'

'You must do as you think right, Superintendent,' said the judge, 'but, as you have thought it right to administer a caution, I think that, for the moment at any rate, my son and daughter should not answer any further questions.'

'Very good, Sir John,' said the Superintendent. 'I quite understand, and, if I may say so, I'm very glad you made the suggestion. I assure you, sir, that this has been the most painful interview in which I have ever taken part.'

A few minutes later the Superintendent and Inspector left. Colonel Brain stayed behind. 'I can't tell you how sorry I am,' he said. 'I wish there were something I could do.'

'That's quite all right, Colonel, you have nothing whatever to reproach yourself with.'

'Haven't I though?' said the colonel. 'If I hadn't talked so much, none of this would have happened. I shall go and make an appreciation and see what I can do. Don't be too despondent. I may have failed the Staff College, but I still get ideas from time to time. I've got one now, as a matter of fact. Good night.'

When he had gone, there was silence for a short time.

'I'm going to have a chat with Bernard,' said the judge. 'Don't say anything to your mother for the moment. She'll have to know later, I'm afraid, if things go wrong.'

'How much can you get for attempted murder?' asked James.·

'There'd be no question of the maximum in a case like this.'

'But what is it?'

'Imprisonment for life.'

CHAPTER TWENTY-ONE

Obstruction

It was unfortunate for the judge and his family and
somewhat ironical that Mr Bean's interest in discomfiting
the judge should have suddenly abated because of his
interview with the Superintendent. If it had abated for
some similar reason before he went to see the
Superintendent – if, for example, someone of sufficient
importance had seriously annoyed him in time – the
verdict on Sidney York would have ended the matter and
neither the judge nor his children would have had to
worry any more about it. But now what Mr Bean thought
or wanted made no difference, for the wheels of the law
had been set in motion. In minor matters it may be
possible for a projected prosecution to be abandoned at
the whim of the man who had been instigating it, but not
in attempted murder. Mr Bean had, indeed, finished with
the judge. He was no longer interested, but his work was
bound to outlive his interest, and, though he and his
sleuths retired from the scene, the Beverley family now
had something far more formidable to contend with than
the lunatic malice of Mr Bean – namely the sense of duty
of the Superintendent at Pemberton and the slow but
certain grinding of the machinery of the law.

But, as far as Mr Bean's new vendetta against the Superintendent was concerned, there was an unexpected development. In the language of the old but excellent story, 'the horse blew first.' In other words, Mr Bean suddenly found himself summoned on a charge of obstruction for leaving his car in Pemberton High Street. If he had been angry before, he was in a fury now. The whole of the resources of Clarion Newspapers Ltd were brought to bear on the Pemberton police force and, in particular, the Superintendent. And to little avail. The charge was duly proceeded with and, in due course, it was heard before the Pemberton magistrates. Mr Bean treated this prosecution for a very minor offence extremely seriously. He would fight it tooth and nail. He had not been guilty of any obstruction, it was a pure piece of vindictiveness on the part of the Superintendent and he could prove it. Through Messrs Rounce and Ponsonby he engaged Mr Gillingham to defend him. Mr Gillingham did not normally do criminal work, and he had certainly not appeared to defend anyone against such a charge for very many years, but for a fee of one hundred and fifty guineas his clerk allowed (or, rather, told) him to do it. He arrived at the court in plenty of time, and his treatment there was what Mr Wyndham had hoped for at the inquest. The Clerk to the Justices had been told that he was appearing and he came and spoke to him before the Justices sat.

'My name's Sittingbourne,' he said. 'I'm the Clerk to the Justices.'

'How d'you do?' said Mr Gillingham.

'The Justices are proposing to take your case first, if that is convenient for you,' said Mr Sittingbourne.

'That's extremely kind of you and them,' said Mr Gillingham. 'I am most grateful. It's really quite extraordinary the courtesy which is shown to one in the courts – when one has a certain status, of course. The other day the Master of the Rolls took a case out of the list simply for my convenience – my own personal convenience, you know. And it wasn't because I was appearing in the House of Lords, you know – which is normally the reason for counsel making such an application on personal grounds. And, of course, I didn't say it was. I told their Lordships quite frankly that it would be highly inconvenient for me to appear in the case that week and that I considered it vital in the interests of my client that I should represent him. "If you say that," said the Master of the Rolls, "I think we can make an exception in your case. The appeal will not be heard this week. Would a day next week be convenient?" And, d'you know,' went on Mr Gillingham, 'they actually fixed a day the following week to suit my special convenience. Almost unheard of, I should say. I suppose they might have done it for FE or Carson. But I must say I'm very grateful to you. It would be a great help if I could get away soon. I've an important conference with the Solicitor-General. And I've been told the Minister of Health wants to consult me about something. I'm not the Treasury junior, you know, but they want to take me in specially, as the matter's unusually complicated.'

'Well – I'm very glad we can accommodate you,' said Mr Sittingbourne. 'We don't often have such distinguished advocates down here.'

'I don't suppose you do,' said Mr Gillingham affably. 'But I'm delighted to come, I assure you.'

'Perhaps you'd like to know who are on the Bench today. Lady Rainham is Chairman and Mr Newington and Mr Faversham are sitting with her.'

'Thank you,' said Mr Gillingham. 'What does she like to be called? I used to find in my early days when I went occasionally to a police court – they were called police courts in those days – I used to find, if the magistrate or chairman had a title, he sometimes preferred to be called "Sir George" to "Your Worship." '

'Ah,' said Mr Sittingbourne, 'you won't find Lady Rainham minds what you call her. She's rather a forthright person, if I may say so. No airs or graces.'

'Well, that's most kind of you,' said Mr Gillingham.

A few minutes later the Justices came in, and the proceedings began.

'Alexander Bean,' called Mr Sittingbourne, and stated the charge against him. Mr Gillingham at once stood up, said that his client pleaded 'not guilty' and sat down again.

'Where is Mr Bean?' asked Lady Rainham.

'He's sitting in front of me,' said Mr Gillingham.

'Well, let him sit in the normal place, please,' said Lady Rainham, 'in front of the dock. That's the custom of this court.'

Mr Bean made a mental note of Lady Rainham for reduction to the ranks, and, flushing slightly, got up and went to his place in front of the dock.

'That's better,' said Lady Rainham. 'Now we can have a good look at him.'

Mr Bean glared at her and forgot all about the Superintendent for the moment.

PC Grimes then went into the witness box and took the oath, and said who he was.

'Are you doing this yourself?' asked Mr Sittingbourne of PC Grimes.

'Yes, sir,' said the witness.

'The defendant is represented by distinguished counsel. Do the police not desire to be represented?' asked Mr

Sittingbourne, looking at the Superintendent who was sitting in Court.

'No, thank you, sir,' said the Superintendent. He knew his bench.

'Very well,' said Mr Sittingbourne. 'Yes, Constable?'

'Your Worships,' began the constable, 'on the 23rd June last, at 3.30 p.m. I was on duty in the High Street, when I saw a large car, index number AAA1, standing outside Packham's Stores. I put a chalk mark on the front wheel and continued to proceed on my beat. At 4 p.m. on the same day I found the car still in the same position. I could tell from the chalk mark that it had not been moved. Both when I first saw the car and when I saw it later, traffic was quite heavy, and, as Your Worships know, the road narrows at that particular point. The result was that traffic each way was considerably impeded. I tried to find the driver, but without avail, until at 4.12 he came to the car and I spoke to him. I recognise the defendant as the man I spoke to. I said,' and the constable, who had a notebook in front of him, was about to read from it, when Mr Gillingham intervened.

'Were those notes made at the time?'

'No,' said the witness, with surprising frankness. 'They were mainly written up next day at the police station.'

'Why didn't you write them the same day?' asked Mr Sittingbourne.

'I was prevented from doing so at the actual time of the occurrence,' said the witness, 'as I had to sort out the traffic which was badly jammed owing to the presence of the defendant's car. When I got back to the station, I was sent on special duty, in consequence of which I couldn't write my notes until the next day.'

'Well – put them away then,' said Mr Sittingbourne. 'Tell us what was said to the best of your recollection.'

'I said to the defendant: "Is this your car, sir?" He said: "It is." I said: "Are you aware that it has been left here for forty-two minutes?" He said: "I haven't timed it, but why shouldn't I leave it there? Haven't you anything better to do than take down car numbers like small boys do with railway engines?" I said: "Your car is causing an obstruction. You can see it for yourself." He said: "It's not my car, but the one over there. Why don't you take its number?" I said: "I have taken its number." That case is before the bench next Monday, your Worships.'

'Never mind about that,' said Mr Sittingbourne. 'Get on with the evidence.'

'I took his particulars and told him he would be reported for a summons. He said: "Did the Superintendent tell you to do this?" I said: "Yes, sir." He said: "I might have known it." He then drove off.'

Mr Gillingham got up to cross-examine.

'This is a busy street?' he asked.

'Yes, sir.'

'Was the car where you first saw it in such a position as to be likely to cause a serious obstruction?'

'Yes, sir.'

'So that traffic would be seriously inconvenienced?'

'Yes, sir.'

'Then why didn't you look for the driver at 3.30 instead of waiting till 4 p.m?'

'I didn't know how long the car had been there, sir.'

'That may be – but is your object to keep the road clear or to secure convictions?'

'Both, sir,' said the constable, with the engaging frankness he had shown before.

'I take it, then, you're out to secure a conviction in this case?'

'I'm out to place the facts before the court, sir.'

'Are you sure of your facts? I suppose you get a lot of these cases?'

'A fair number, sir.'

'As you didn't make up your notes till next day, you could have made a mistake, couldn't you?'

'I could have, sir, but I didn't.'

'Why are you so sure?'

'Because I knew Mr Bean by name, sir, and I was struck by the number of the car.'

'You said that you told the defendant that the Superintendent had told you to take his particulars. How did that come about?'

'The Superintendent told us all, sir, that we must keep the High Street clear of obstruction and that the driver of any car which stayed in certain places in the High Street longer than ten minutes between certain hours must be summoned.'

'Whether there was an actual obstruction or not?'

'Yes, sir. May I add something?'

'Well – what is it?'

'You couldn't leave a car at any of those places in the High Street at those times without causing an obstruction, sir.'

Mr Gillingham had long sensed that this was a hopeless case, but he decided to give Mr Bean his money's worth and he continued to cross-examine the constable for another quarter of an hour. Eventually he sat down.

'That's the case, your Worships,' said the constable.

'With your Worships' leave,' said Mr Gillingham, 'I will open the case for the defence and address you again at the end of the evidence. I am calling two witnesses.'

'I beg your pardon?' said Lady Rainham.

Mr Gillingham repeated what he had said.

213

'Well, really!' said Lady Rainham. 'I thought this was a case of obstruction in the High Street. We don't want to make a Tichborne case of it, do we?'

'Alleged obstruction,' said Mr Gillingham.

'Alleged obstruction,' repeated Lady Rainham, emphasising the word 'alleged' and then emphasising even more the word 'obstruction,' and adding, with even greater emphasis, 'in the High Street.'

'The 1948 Act gives me a right,' persisted Mr Gillingham, 'to choose whether I will address you before or after calling my evidence – '

'Choose away,' interrupted Lady Rainham.

'But,' continued Mr Gillingham, 'with your permission, I can address you twice.'

'Without intending any disrespect to you,' replied Lady Rainham, 'we are only too well aware of that. Moreover, if we let you speak twice, the prosecution can have another go as well.' She paused, and then: 'You see, I have read the 1948 Act,' she added.

'Of course,' said Mr Gillingham.

'No "of course" at all,' said Lady Rainham, 'but Mr Sittingbourne made me. Now, shall we get on, please? We've a lot of other work to do – including several more cases of obstruction – alleged obstruction in the High Street – which is also a busy place.'

'Have I your permission to address you twice?' persisted Mr Gillingham.

'Oh – this is tiresome,' said Lady Rainham. 'We shouldn't have taken your case first if we'd known all this was going to happen. To begin with, you cross-examined the police officer as though your client were charged with burglary or arson or even worse. We don't like people leaving cars in the narrow part of the High Street – indeed, I should have thought that no one with any sense would dream of leaving a car there – but we shan't order your client to be hanged if we convict him, you know. It's a silly, inconsiderate thing – alleged thing – to do, but it's not all that bad. Provided your client pays the fine, he won't even go to prison, you know. Aren't you making rather too heavy weather of this little affair?'

'My client is entitled to have his case presented as fully and carefully as if he were charged with any other crime.'

'As carefully, if you like,' said Lady Rainham, 'but not as fully. If he were charged with shoplifting, we'd certainly give you two speeches, but not in a simple case of obstruction. After all, either he left his car there or he didn't, and either it was there for the time the officer said or it wasn't. And that's all there is to it.'

'With respect, it isn't, your Worship,' said Mr Gillingham. 'The question is whether the car caused an obstruction.'

'Have you been to the place?' said Lady Rainham, with a sigh.

'Yes, I have,' said Mr Gillingham.

'Have you been to it at 3.30 on a Saturday?'

'I can't say that I have.'

'Well, if we should happen to convict your client, I suggest you should come one Saturday. There's quite a good service of trains.'

At this stage Mr Bean interrupted. 'It's quite obvious there's no point in going on with the case before such an obviously biased bench,' he said. 'What's the fine?'

'Forty shillings,' said Lady Rainham, 'is the usual charge, and, subject to the opinion of my colleagues, we won't add anything for your making such a silly fuss about it.' She glanced to the right and the left, received the necessary nods and added brightly: 'Yes, forty shillings, please. We're delighted to have such distinguished visitors, but do be more careful another time, please. Thank you, Mr Gillingham. Good morning. Call the next case please, Mr Sittingbourne.'

Mr Bean left the Court at once. He did not wait to thank Mr Gillingham or Mr Rounce. He was in despair. During his life he had dealt with difficult problems in a masterly manner, he had faced gravely threatening setbacks, and prevented serious disasters, he had formed Clarion Newspapers Ltd and made it the largest newspaper company the British Isles had ever known. In every matter which he considered important he had, when he had wanted, always defeated his adversaries. And now, because he had been, as he thought, made a fool of by the Pemberton Bench and fined forty shillings for obstruction in the High Street, life was not worth living. But so it is with lunatics of his kind. He went straight to one of his country houses, took a shotgun, loaded it and was about to shoot himself. But, just before he pressed the trigger, he tried to visualise the obituary notices about himself, and he paused for a moment to think of them. That pause was fatal to his resolve. He suddenly had an intense desire to read his obituary notices. He put away the shotgun, raced up to London in his car, and sent for his Editor.

'Frank,' he said, 'the doctors tell me I've a weak heart. Might pop off at any moment.'

'I'm terribly sorry to hear that. You should have a rest.'

'Oh – no – it's as good a way of dying as any. Now – look – I'd like to see what you're going to say about me when I've gone. So have a notice set up now – headlines and everything – you can leave out the cause of death and, if I'm run over or anything, you can change the headlines. But I want to see what it looks like. Now, I'm trusting you, Frank. I want what you'll really say – nothing fancy dished up for my benefit. Will you do it?'

'Of course, if you want, but I'd rather not.'

'Well – I do want – and don't forget – a true bill, Frank – I trust you, mind you.'

'All right,' said the Editor, and he got down to it. To Frank's surprise, Mr Bean did not instantly dismiss him when he read his obituary notice. On the contrary, he thanked him warmly. 'I knew I could trust you,' he said. 'D'you know, I think it's done my heart good. I think I shall live quite a bit longer.'

One of the passages in the notice read as follows: 'He never received the knighthood he so ardently desired and for which he had worked so hard.'

Mr Bean decided to live in order to receive it. That, in his view, was the only way in which he could get even with Frank.

CHAPTER TWENTY-TWO

Untruth at Last

While Colonel Brain was giving effect to his idea, the judge was talking to Bernard.

'It's my fault, Bernard,' he said. 'Entirely mine. If I'd never become a judge, this would not have happened. I'd have had a larger income, too, if I'd stayed at the Bar.'

'Anyone would have done the same,' said Bernard. There was silence for a moment and then he added: 'I suppose there'll be no question of Judy being convicted.'

'My dear boy – I'm afraid there's every possibility.'

'But surely innocent people don't get convicted of serious crime in this country today.'

The judge hesitated a moment before saying: 'No, Bernard, they don't.'

'But, good heavens, you're not suggesting Judy knew anything about this?'

'What else can I suggest?'

'She's told me herself that she knew nothing about it.'

'I suppose it's natural she should say that to you.'

'But I know she wasn't lying. She hasn't told me everything. She couldn't, to protect Jimmy, but I know she was telling me the truth.'

'But – ' began the judge, 'but – Jimmy has assured me he had nothing to do with it. They can't both be telling the truth. I'm afraid it only goes to show that they were both in it.'

'But why should she lie to me?'

'Or Jimmy to me?'

They were walking in the garden. Suddenly the judge stopped.

'We must see them at once,' he said.

'What is it?'

'Never mind. Come at once.'

They went and found James and Judy. 'Now, look,' said the judge, 'you're in a mess, I'm in a mess, we're all in a mess. But there is just a possibility. But it'll be no good unless you both tell me the truth and the whole truth, irrespective of how you think it may hurt the other. Will you do it? Will you answer my questions without hesitation and without concealing or distorting anything? Well, James?'

James hesitated. Then: 'I suppose you know best, Father. All right, I will.'

'Judy?' said the judge.

'I don't know,' she said.

'Please,' said Bernard, 'I want you to. It must be the right thing to do.'

'All right,' said Judy.

'Now, Jimmy, did you take the lamp out?'

'No.'

Judy looked at him.

'Where did you find it?'

'In Judy's bag.'

'Had you seen it before?'

'Never – so far as I know.'

'Now, Judy, did you take it out?'

'No.'

'Where did you find it?'

219

'In a bowl in the lounge under Jimmy's hat. I thought he'd taken it. So I stuffed it into my bag.'

'Oh – my God – ' said James.

No one said anything for a moment. Then Judy fainted. The joy at the sudden discovery was too much for her. When she came to a minute later, her father was speaking.

'There's no time for fainting,' he said, 'there's a lot to be done. You're not out of the wood by a long way yet. With the evidence the Superintendent has, I very much doubt if he'll stop a prosecution just because you both suddenly tell the truth. We must go and see him at the earliest possible moment. But don't be too hopeful.'

'But they'll never be convicted after they've explained everything, will they? They couldn't be,' said Bernard.

'Maybe not,' said the judge. 'But, thinking of myself for the moment – it'll be just as bad for me if there's a prosecution at all. The story of York and the court martial is almost bound to come out. And, even as far as James and Judy are concerned, there's a substantial body of evidence against them. It's all very well to come along now and try to explain it away. However, that's what we must do. We must go first thing in the morning.'

At about the same time as the judge and Bernard had discovered that James and Judy were both entirely innocent, Colonel Brain was being dealt with by his housekeeper.

'Ginger pop, indeed,' she was saying. 'D'you think I don't know the smell of whisky?'

'Apparently not,' said the colonel, slowly and thickly but with conviction. 'The basis was ginger pop. As to that I could take an oath – an oath, I say.'

'Well, you're drunk anyway.'

'As to that,' said the colonel, 'I should not be prepared to take an oath. I will make a statement from where I stand. Then I can't be cross-examined.'

'Can't you?' said his housekeeper. 'What d'you want to go and get drunk for? Tell me that.'

'Without the slightest admission, my dear lady,' said the colonel, 'without even a suspicion of an admission – that's pretty good – even when you're sober – without the slightest suspicion of a – something gone wrong there, I'm afraid – try again – without – '

'Will you tell me what it's about or not?' interrupted the lady. 'I shan't take your boots off till you have.'

'In that case,' said the colonel, with as much dignity as he could muster, 'in that case I will tell you. But I must make it plain that the statement is obtained from me by threats and cannot be used in evidence – positively not – see *Manual of Military Law* page – page – now that's a funny thing – I'll get it.'

'You'll stay where you are. Come along now.'

'Very well, my dear lady, you must take my word for it. It's at the top of page – well never mind. Under duress – a fellow must have his boots off – under duress, I repeat, well, it was like this. I wanted old Cumberland to do something for me. He said "No." I said "Yes." He said "No" again. And then I had an idea. I offered him a whisky. "Not unless *you* do," says he. "But, my dear fellow," I said, "I hate the stuff. Everyone knows that." "All right," he says, "then make it ginger pop – with gin." The sting in the tail, you see. And, to cut a long story short – and have my boots off – it was the ginger pop – with gin – that did it. The old boy was so impressed at the way I took the stuff that he agreed, and the battle was over – and, my dear lady, I never had to use my reserves.'

'But what did he agree to do?'

'As to that, dear lady, wild horses could not drag it out of me.'

'All right,' said the lady, 'but you'll need someone to help you off with your boots.'

On the following day the judge and Bernard, James and Judy made an early appointment to see the Superintendent.

'There's been a terrible mistake,' said the judge. 'My son thought my daughter was responsible and she thought he was. Hence some of their statements, but the truth is now quite plain. I invite you to listen to what they say and ask them any questions you wish about the matter.'

'Very well,' said the Superintendent, 'but you will, of course, understand, Sir John, that anything they say may be used in evidence.'

James and Judy then explained in full what had happened from the time they had been told by their father about Sidney York. The Superintendent asked them a few questions and then said: 'Well, I quite follow, Sir John, what Mr Beverley and Miss Beverley have told me and I'm not saying it isn't correct but it still doesn't explain how the lamp came to be in the bowl. Mr Cumberland was quite positive that he'd put it in the socket. He had only just changed it. Are you suggesting anyone else can have taken it out? It hardly seems likely.'

'Cumberland could have made a mistake.'

'Of course he could. But he says he hasn't. Won't it be for the jury to say if his evidence is right or not? You see – there's a horrible series of coincidences if he's making a mistake. It is so very unfortunate not only that he should make such a mistake but that both Mr Beverley and Miss Beverley should make such mistakes. Very unfortunate, too, that there should have been good reason for wanting Sidney York out of the way and that Colonel Brain should have suggested – jocularly, it's true – a method of doing it. Surely, Sir John, you'd have to leave such a case to the jury?'

'I agree that there is evidence, Superintendent. The question is whether it's fit to be submitted to a jury. That's for you to say.'

'Well, it isn't really, Sir John. I shall have to send all this material to the Director, including, of course, these latest statements. It will be for him to say if there's to be a prosecution – but wouldn't you yourself, sir, say that it's a case that ought to be tried, whatever you might think the ultimate result would be? Quite candidly, sir, no one would be more pleased than I should be if the Director turned it down, but I can't think it likely, can you, sir?' and he turned to Bernard.

'I suppose not,' said Bernard. 'There is a lot of evidence. But, of course, it ultimately depends on Cumberland. If he's making a mistake the whole thing goes.'

'I agree, but he says he isn't. He's quite sure about it.'

At that moment, the telephone in the Superintendent's room rang. He answered it. 'Yes?' he said 'Who? Oh – oh – tell them to wait, please.'

He replaced the receiver and turned to his visitors. 'It's Colonel Brain and Mr and Mrs Cumberland to see me,' he said. 'Perhaps you wouldn't mind waiting in this other room while I see them.' A minute later Colonel Brain and Mr and Mrs Cumberland were shown in to the Superintendent.

'Well,' he asked, 'what can I do for you?'

'Superintendent,' said the colonel, 'we've come to correct a bad mistake.'

'Oh – what is it?' asked the Superintendent.

'Tell the Superintendent,' said the colonel to Mr Cumberland.

223

Mr Cumberland hesitated for a moment and then said: 'I made a mistake about the lamp.'

'What!' said the Superintendent.

'Yes,' said Mr Cumberland. 'My memory isn't as good as it was. I know I told you that I put the lamp in, but I remember now that I didn't.'

'Indeed?' said the Superintendent. 'But you were quite sure when you told me before.'

'My wife will tell you that I'm often quite sure when I'm wrong.'

'Are you now quite sure,' asked the Superintendent, 'that you forgot to put the lamp in?'

'Quite sure,' said Mr Cumberland.

'And I suppose your wife will now tell me,' said the Superintendent, 'that you are wrong.'

'To tell you the truth,' began Mrs Cumberland.

'Yes,' said the Superintendent. 'I should like the truth.'

'To tell you the truth – I never know whether he's right or wrong. As I told you in the first place, I never saw him put it in.'

'Yes – that's quite true,' said the Superintendent, 'you did say that.'

'I left him with it in his hand. I'd also told him to do one or two things – get out a bill for someone, I think was one of them, and he might have put it down and forgotten about it.'

'Then where is it?' asked the Superintendent.

Colonel Brain intervened.

'My dear fellow, that is a strange thing that it can't be found. But, if I may say so, I've known a good many things stranger than that. I remember once – '

'Please, Colonel,' interrupted the Superintendent, 'another time, if you don't mind.'

'But it might help you, my dear fellow.'

'No need, thank you. In fact we know where the lamp is. If you'll look in the junk cupboard, just off the lounge, you'll find it there.'

'Then everything's cleared up, is it?' said the colonel.

'I didn't say everything was cleared up. I said we knew where the lamp was. And we know part of its history before that. But we don't know what Mr Cumberland did with it, if he didn't put it in its right place. Unless you can tell us, of course?'

'Well – I don't rightly know,' said Mr Cumberland. 'But I can say that I didn't put it in the socket over the stairs. I reproach myself very much – first, for not having put it there; secondly, for telling you that I did.'

'You wouldn't have put it in the bowl in the lounge by any chance, I suppose?' asked the Superintendent.

'Well, you know,' said Mr Cumberland, 'I might very well have done. Come to think of it now, that's where I did put it.'

'You're quite sure of that, are you, Mr Cumberland?'

'Oh – yes, thank you – quite sure – now you've reminded me. That's where it was I put it.'

'Well,' said the Superintendent, 'if you'll just sign a statement to that effect, I think that will be all, thank you. And I may say I'm very much obliged to you. A lot of things might have happened if you hadn't come and told me that. But now I don't think they'll be necessary. Thank you very much indeed.'

The Superintendent was extremely pleased.

After Mr Cumberland had signed the new statement, he and his wife and Colonel Brain left the police station.

'Did I do all right?' asked Mr Cumberland anxiously.

'Fine, my dear fellow, and it didn't feel too bad, did it?'

'Well,' said Mr Cumberland, 'I've never told such a deliberate lie before, but, as you say, it was in a good cause, and I don't think it'll get me into the habit.'

HENRY CECIL

ACCORDING TO THE EVIDENCE

Alec Morland is on trial for murder. He has tried to remedy the ineffectiveness of the law by taking matters into his own hands. Unfortunately for him, his alleged crime was not committed in immediate defence of others or of himself. In this fascinating murder trial you will not find out until the very end just how the law will interpret his actions. Will his defence be accepted or does a different fate await him?

THE ASKING PRICE

Ronald Holbrook is a fifty-seven-year-old bachelor who has lived in the same house for twenty years. Jane Doughty, the daughter of his next-door neighbours, is seventeen. She suddenly decides she is in love with Ronald and wants to marry him. Everyone is amused at first but then events take a disturbingly sinister turn and Ronald finds himself enmeshed in a potentially tragic situation.

'The secret of Mr Cecil's success lies in continuing to do superbly what everyone now knows he can do well.'
The Sunday Times

Henry Cecil

Brief Tales from the Bench

What does it feel like to be a Judge? Read these stories and you can almost feel you are looking at proceedings from the lofty position of the Bench.

With a collection of eccentric and amusing characters, Henry Cecil brings to life the trials in a County Court and exposes the complex and often contradictory workings of the English legal system.

'Immensely readable. His stories rely above all on one quality – an extraordinary, an arresting, a really staggering ingenuity.'
New Statesman

Brothers in Law

Roger Thursby, aged twenty-four, is called to the bar. He is young, inexperienced and his love life is complicated. He blunders his way through a succession of comic adventures including his calamitous debut at the bar.

His career takes an upward turn when he is chosen to defend the caddish Alfred Green at the Old Bailey. In this first Roger Thursby novel Henry Cecil satirizes the legal profession with his usual wit and insight.

'Uproariously funny.' *The Times*

'Full of charm and humour. I think it is the best Henry Cecil yet.' P G Wodehouse

Henry Cecil

Hunt the Slipper

Harriet and Graham have been happily married for twenty years. One day Graham fails to return home and Harriet begins to realise she has been abandoned. This feeling is strengthened when she starts to receive monthly payments from an untraceable source. After five years on her own Harriet begins to see another man and divorces Graham on the grounds of his desertion. Then one evening Harriet returns home to find Graham sitting in a chair, casually reading a book. Her initial relief turns to anger and then to fear when she realises that if Graham's story is true, she may never trust his sanity again. This complex comedy thriller will grip your attention to the very last page.

Sober as a Judge

Roger Thursby, the hero of *Brothers in Law* and *Friends at Court*, continues his career as a High Court judge. He presides over a series of unusual cases, including a professional debtor and an action about a consignment of oranges which turned to juice before delivery. There is a delightful succession of eccentric witnesses as the reader views proceedings from the Bench.

'The author's gift for brilliant characterisation makes this a book that will delight lawyers and laymen as much as did its predecessors.' *The Daily Telegraph*

OTHER TITLES BY HENRY CECIL AVAILABLE DIRECT
FROM HOUSE OF STRATUS

Quantity		£	$(US)	$(CAN)	€
	ACCORDING TO THE EVIDENCE	6.99	11.50	15.99	11.50
	ALIBI FOR A JUDGE	6.99	11.50	15.99	11.50
	THE ASKING PRICE	6.99	11.50	15.99	11.50
	BRIEF TALES FROM THE BENCH	6.99	11.50	15.99	11.50
	BROTHERS IN LAW	6.99	11.50	15.99	11.50
	THE BUTTERCUP SPELL	6.99	11.50	15.99	11.50
	CROSS PURPOSES	6.99	11.50	15.99	11.50
	DAUGHTERS IN LAW	6.99	11.50	15.99	11.50
	FATHERS IN LAW	6.99	11.50	15.99	11.50
	FRIENDS AT COURT	6.99	11.50	15.99	11.50
	FULL CIRCLE	6.99	11.50	15.99	11.50
	HUNT THE SLIPPER	6.99	11.50	15.99	11.50
	INDEPENDENT WITNESS	6.99	11.50	15.99	11.50

ALL HOUSE OF STRATUS BOOKS ARE AVAILABLE FROM GOOD BOOKSHOPS OR
DIRECT FROM THE PUBLISHER:

Internet: www.houseofstratus.com including author interviews, reviews,
features.

Email: sales@houseofstratus.com please quote author, title and credit card
details.

OTHER TITLES BY HENRY CECIL AVAILABLE DIRECT FROM HOUSE OF STRATUS

Quantity		£	$(US)	$(CAN)	€
	MUCH IN EVIDENCE	6.99	11.50	15.99	11.50
	NO BAIL FOR THE JUDGE	6.99	11.50	15.99	11.50
	NO FEAR OR FAVOUR	6.99	11.50	15.99	11.50
	THE PAINSWICK LINE	6.99	11.50	15.99	11.50
	PORTRAIT OF A JUDGE	6.99	11.50	15.99	11.50
	SETTLED OUT OF COURT	6.99	11.50	15.99	11.50
	SOBER AS A JUDGE	6.99	11.50	15.99	11.50
	TELL YOU WHAT I'LL DO	6.99	11.50	15.99	11.50
	TRUTH WITH HER BOOTS ON	6.99	11.50	15.99	11.50
	UNLAWFUL OCCASIONS	6.99	11.50	15.99	11.50
	THE WANTED MAN	6.99	11.50	15.99	11.50
	WAYS AND MEANS	6.99	11.50	15.99	11.50
	A WOMAN NAMED ANNE	6.99	11.50	15.99	11.50

ALL HOUSE OF STRATUS BOOKS ARE AVAILABLE FROM GOOD BOOKSHOPS OR DIRECT FROM THE PUBLISHER:

Hotline: UK ONLY: **0800 169 1780**, please quote author, title and credit card details.
INTERNATIONAL: **+44 (0) 20 7494 6400**, please quote author, title, and credit card details.

Send to: **House of Stratus**
24c Old Burlington Street
London
W1X 1RL
UK

Please allow following carriage costs per ORDER
(For goods up to free carriage limits shown)

	£(Sterling)	$(US)	$(CAN)	€(Euros)
UK	1.95	3.20	4.29	3.00
Europe	2.95	4.99	6.49	5.00
North America	2.95	4.99	6.49	5.00
Rest of World	2.95	5.99	7.75	6.00
Free carriage for goods value over:	50	75	100	75

PLEASE SEND CHEQUE, POSTAL ORDER (STERLING ONLY), EUROCHEQUE, OR
INTERNATIONAL MONEY ORDER (PLEASE CIRCLE METHOD OF PAYMENT YOU WISH TO USE)
MAKE PAYABLE TO: STRATUS HOLDINGS plc

Order total including postage:_____Please tick currency you wish to use and add total amount of order:

☐ £ (Sterling)   ☐ $ (US)   ☐ $ (CAN)   ☐ € (EUROS)

VISA, MASTERCARD, SWITCH, AMEX, SOLO, JCB:

☐☐☐☐☐☐☐☐☐☐☐☐☐☐☐☐☐☐☐☐☐☐☐☐

Issue number (Switch only):

☐☐☐

Start Date: **Expiry Date:**

☐☐/☐☐   ☐☐/☐☐

Signature: _____

NAME: _____

ADDRESS: _____

_____

POSTCODE: _____

Please allow 28 days for delivery.

Prices subject to change without notice.
Please tick box if you do not wish to receive any additional information. ☐

House of Stratus publishes many other titles in this genre; please
check our website (**www.houseofstratus.com**) for more details